C0-BUU-255

WITHDRAWN
University of
Illinois Library
at Urbana-Champaign

65p

The predictive value of CSE grades for further education

I. C. Williams

N. C. Boreham

Evans / Methuen Educational

First published 1971 for the Schools Council
by Evans Brothers Limited
Montague House, Russell Square, London WC1B 5BX
and Methuen Educational Limited
11 New Fetter Lane, London EC4P 4EE

Distributed in the US by Citation Press
Scholastic Magazines Inc., 50 West 44th Street
New York, N Y 10036

© Schools Council Publications 1972

All rights reserved. No part of this publication
may be reproduced or transmitted, in any form
or by any means, electronic, mechanical, photocopying,
recording or otherwise without the
prior permission of the publishers.

SBN 423 46540 6

Printed in Great Britain by
Richard Clay (The Chaucer Press) Ltd
Bungay, Suffolk

Contents

371. 27
W 672 p
cop. 2

Foreword   *page* 5

I   **Origins of the project**   7

II   **Research design**   9

III **Results**   15
     1. Mechanical engineering technicians course, part I   15
     2. Electrical technicians course, part I   23
     3. General course in engineering   30
     4. Basic engineering craft studies course
        (mechanical bias)   38
     5. General catering course   48
     6. Ladies' hairdressing course   56
     7. Shorthand-typists' certificate, stage II   61
     8. Secretarial duties, stage II   66

IV   **General conclusions**   74

     Appendices
     A   Supplementary tables   77
     B   Explanation of some of the statistical terms used   84
     C   CSE subjects included in the research   86

     Members of the consultative committee   87

LIBRARY U. OF I. URBANA-CHAMPAIGN

Foreword

The Schools Council is pleased to make available in the Examinations Bulletin series this study of the predictive value for further education of grades achieved in the Certificate of Secondary Education.

The project, which was based at Thurrock Technical College, was under the direction of the then Principal of the College, Mr I. C. Williams, with Mr N. C. Boreham as project organizer.

With a wide readership in mind, the presentation of each section of the chief results follows an identical format, chosen for this purpose, consisting of a summary of findings, diagrammatic representation, and analyses of data with relevant tabulation and comment. It is hoped that this procedure will ensure that the maximum use will be made of the findings by teachers, both in schools and in further education, by examining boards, and by those responsible for the selection and placement of further education students.

The Council offers its sincere thanks to the colleges, which, at very short notice in 1969, gave details of students' CSE qualifications and performance in that summer's further education examinations, and for additional information provided in the early months of 1970. The Council is grateful also to the students who completed questionnaires and to the CSE examining boards, the City and Guilds of London Institute, and the Royal Society of Arts for their co-operation with the project.

I. Origins of the project

> ... it has been clearly in our minds throughout that these [the CSE] examinations might be of value in the selection of candidates for further education courses. The need for careful selection in this field is becoming increasingly evident in view of the growing range and diversity of the courses that are being made available ... we would hope that those in technical colleges who are concerned with placing students, and who would therefore make use of these examinations, would treat them as no more than one piece of evidence amongst others, and would continue to take account of school courses followed, of school reports, the results of interviews, and other such information.*

This forecast in the Beloe Report that CSE results would be used in the selection and placement of further education students has been fulfilled. From the earliest days of CSE, many college principals, employers, and careers officers welcomed the new examination as a supplementary source of information for allocating students to craft and technician courses and to industrial apprenticeships. The most notable development took place in Coventry, where R. A. Arculus, Principal of Coventry Technical College, in conjunction with a local headmaster (a former member of the Beloe Committee and a member of the West Midlands CSE Board), together with representatives of the schools and industry, examined the relevance of the various CSE grades for further education courses. The 'Coventry Document' which emerged from these deliberations, and which was to be revised in each successive year, remains the most authoritative prediction of the predictive values of CSE grades for further education courses, and is used by schools and technical colleges, careers advisers, and employers. It was made extensively available to industry when the British Association for Commercial and Industrial Education published, in March 1966, *The Certificate of Secondary Education: its Scope and Significance*, by P. Walton and R. A. Arculus. Industry's growing interest in the uses of the various CSE grades was made manifest in a paper, 'CSE: the user's view', submitted to the CSE sub-committee in January 1969 (unpublished).

The project, authorized by the Schools Council in 1968 and completed in 1970, aims to estimate how effectively CSE is able to serve as a supplementary source of information for the allocation of students to courses at the crafts and technician levels in colleges of further education.

* *Secondary School Examinations other than the GCE:* Report of a Committee Appointed by the Secondary School Examinations Council (HMSO, 1960), paras 131 and 133.

Two major needs for this research were evident. First, it had been difficult to obtain samples large enough to make possible validation studies of the suggested entry requirements. There was in consequence much uncertainty about the significance of the various grades, and indeed about whether CSE possessed predictive validity at all. Second, with the increasing acceptance of the comparability between grade 1 and a pass at the ordinary level of the GCE, the lower CSE grades were coming to be regarded in some quarters as 'fail grades'. If the lower grades could be defined in terms of suitability for certain further education courses, it was thought, candidates and their parents would be more aware of the positive levels of attainment represented by these grades.

II. Research design

A project to investigate all the questions raised by the use of CSE for predicting college performance would have required more time and resources than were available. In planning the research, therefore, a decision had to be made about what kind of information was most needed, so that a programme of research could be chosen that would be both feasible and useful. The general problem of the predictive validity of CSE for further education can be resolved into a number of interrelated but distinguishable problems:

a   How many of the students in further education took CSE at school? And are the subjects with predictive validity those which have been taken by the majority of the students? The usefulness of CSE for prediction depends on factors other than its validity. If the best predictors are minority subjects, their use will not substantially increase the number of students whose further education performance can be accurately predicted.

b   If CSE has predictive value, in which sectors of further education is it most useful? There are more than two hundred further education courses open to school-leavers who obtained CSE grades lower than grade 1. Different courses call for different abilities: it is by no means certain that the information about pupils' attainment provided by CSE results will be valuable as a predictor for all these courses.

c   Which CSE subjects are the best predictors for each further education course? The range of subjects that may be taken for CSE is wide. It is open to question whether the procedure of requiring minimum grades without specifying in which subjects they are to be obtained is a justifiable procedure for predicting college performance from CSE results.

d   Do the students who took CSE at school perform significantly better in college than those who left school at fifteen? This is essentially a problem of isolating the effect of the extra year in school from other factors which influence college performance, and determining its value as a preparation for further study.

e   Does the predictive information supplied by CSE add to what can be learnt from headmasters' reports, diagnostic tests, and interviews? Even if CSE provides predictive information, the same information may be more readily available from other sources such as these.

f   If CSE results do provide unique predictive information, what weight should be attached to them when predicting college performance? Before

9

the full significance of CSE can be known it will be necessary to learn the relative importance of CSE and factors not measured by CSE, such as special abilities and motivation towards a vocationally orientated course.

g   CSE syllabuses for subjects with the same title differ widely. Do different syllabuses have different value in preparing pupils for further education?

The area of uncertainty towards which this research was directed comprised the first three problems described above. The questions for which it sought answers were these:

a   Could anything have been inferred from students' CSE grades about their chances of success in any of a number of further education courses?

b   If so, which CSE subjects were the best predictors for each course?

c   What probability of success was associated with each grade in these subjects?

Methods*

The method employed was to compare students' performance in the CSE examinations with their subsequent performance in further education. A high correlation between grades in a CSE subject and further education performance would imply that the CSE subject concerned could be used to predict students' further education results. CSE subjects were investigated as possible predictors in two ways: each subject as a single predictive measure, and combinations of two subjects as multiple predictors. (Students who had taken any given combination of three or more subjects were too few to enable 'batteries' of more than two to be considered.) The subjects chosen for investigation were those that had been taken by the greatest number of students. The combinations to be investigated were chosen according to two criteria: that a sufficient number of students had grades in both subjects, and that the students successful in further education had on average obtained higher CSE grades than those who were unsuccessful.

The overall aim was to identify the best predictors for each further education course. Comparison of the strength of the correlations obtained for different subjects was a somewhat uncertain procedure, for the students had not all taken the same subjects, resulting in distinct, albeit overlapping samples. An additional complication here was that students had sometimes been selected by reference to some but not all the CSE subjects under investigation. Although in some cases a direct comparison of correlation coefficients might be unreliable, it was, however, possible to see where a shrinkage effect might have occurred, and to modify the interpretations accordingly. After identifying the best predictors of each course, grades in these subjects were evaluated in terms of what they implied about success in further education.

* An explanation of some of the statistical terms used in this report is given in Appendix B.

10

To determine the degree of success attained by students in further education, it was necessary to make reference to external examinations: the students' level of achievement in further education was defined for the purposes of the research as their level of achievement in the final examination. The aim of the research in the case of the technician and commerce courses was to test whether CSE grades could have been used to predict which students would pass and which would fail. This procedure was not adopted in the case of the craft courses, however, for the examinations in these subjects have a high pass rate. The aim when investigating the craft courses was to test whether CSE grades could have been used to distinguish the students who passed with credit or distinction from those who did not reach this standard. Most of the latter group obtained a pass, and were of course in no sense unsuccessful. However, it was thought that it would be a useful predictive function to be able to distinguish the 'high flyers' from the others. The use of predictive information is not restricted to selection; knowledge of which students were likely to have more difficulty than usual in completing the course could be of use to colleges in arranging 'bridge courses' and similar remedial programmes. The general course in engineering presented a special case, for by performing well enough on this course students can qualify for the Ordinary National scheme. The aim here, then, was to test whether CSE grades could have been used to predict which students would qualify for entry to a course leading to the Ordinary National Certificate or Diploma.

It was decided to restrict the research to courses leading to the examinations of the City and Guilds of London Institute and the Royal Society of Arts, thereby ensuring that the criterion of further education performance would be comparable between colleges. Examination results were a valid criterion by which to measure further education achievement, for the objectives of the courses studied in the research are more closely allied to the aim of obtaining a qualification than those in other sectors of education. In this connexion, however, an important limitation to the findings of this project should be noted. Technical education is a dual process involving the student in both an employer's training scheme and a more theoretical course of study at college. The criterion used in this research is primarily an educational one, a measure of success at college. Little is known of its relationship with job performance, and so the results given in this report relate only indirectly to the students' suitability for the careers that they eventually hoped to pursue.

Further education courses investigated

It was inevitable that the scope of the project should be restricted to a small number of courses. In the light of the following considerations, eight were chosen for investigation. According to its terms of reference, the project was to

11

be concerned chiefly with CSE grades lower than 1: this focused the research on the craft and technician level, the sector of further education which school-leavers with the lower CSE grades usually enter. In addition it was decided to concentrate on the courses that, for most students, would be their first period of study in further education, such as the part I and general courses. It is for these that a record of school performance is most likely to have importance as a predictor, rather than for those preceded by other further education courses in the same field. A third consideration was that if the results were to be of general interest, the most popular courses were to be preferred, and an attempt made to ensure that the major subject areas were all represented. Brief details of the courses chosen are given in the following sections.

Mechanical engineering technicians, part I (City and Guilds subject 293). The purpose of this course is to qualify mechanical engineering apprentices for positions of responsibility, such as supervisory roles, plant maintenance, shop and process control, or drawing office practice. Although the part I certificate is a qualification complete in itself, the course is designed as the first part of a continuous training scheme. The syllabus includes workshop processes and practice, engineering drawing and materials, and engineering science and mathematics. The examination consists of an externally-marked written paper in each of these three subjects. Most students attend a two-year, day-release course sponsored by their employers.

Electrical technicians, part I (City and Guilds subject 57). This course is similar in standard to the mechanical technicians' course, providing a qualification for technicians engaged in the design, manufacture, and operation of electrical plant and equipment. The examination consists of three externally-marked papers in engineering materials and drawing, electrical engineering principles, and practical mathematics.

General course in engineering (City and Guilds subject 287). This course is intended for school-leavers who show promise of being able to undertake either an Ordinary National course or a technician course. Its objectives are to provide a common grounding for further study in all branches of engineering, and to diagnose whether students are capable of proceeding to an Ordinary National course. The syllabus includes engineering science, mathematics, workshop processes, and engineering drawing. The examination, which is of approximately GCE O-level standard, consists of one written paper in each of these four subjects. The 'G-course' is usually taken in one year, but may in some circumstances be taken in two.

Basic engineering craft studies (City and Guilds subject 500). A one-year course providing a common grounding for subsequent and more specialized craft training. The examination consists of a common core paper taken by all candidates and a

12

'bias' paper which concentrates on one of the branches of engineering. All the students in the sample had taken the mechanical bias paper.

General catering (City and Guilds subject 441). A one-year, full-time course giving the school-leaver a general introduction to catering, as a preparation for more specialized courses in this subject. The syllabus has a bias towards practical training rather than academic study, covering all aspects of food preparation, food service, and accommodation services. The examination consists of two externally-marked written papers, together with a college assessment of the student's success in mastering practical skills, and a written project, which is also marked by the college.

Ladies' hairdressing (City and Guilds subject 263). A course which may be taken full-time in two years or part-time by hairdressing apprentices in three. Designed to teach the basic skills of hairdressing, the course also includes design and relevant aspects of elementary science. The examination comprises three written papers, in ladies' hairdressing, science, and design, together with a four-hour practical test. All are assessed externally.

Shorthand-typists' certificate, stage II (Royal Society of Arts). The examination consists of recording in shorthand and later typing a number of passages dictated at 80 words per minute, typing a fair copy from a draft, and a test of English spelling, punctuation, and vocabulary. This course is usually taken as part of a full-time course including other commercial subjects.

Secretarial duties, stage II (Royal Society of Arts). A course designed to introduce the intending secretary to commercial organization, office practice, and the methods and machinery of carrying out a wide range of secretarial duties. It is usually taken as part of a full-time course including other commercial subjects.

The sample

The population with which the research was concerned consisted of the students who had taken CSE while at school and who entered colleges of further education during the sessions 1968/9 and 1969/70 to study on the courses described above, taking the final examinations in these subjects in the summer of 1970.

Difficulties were encountered in constructing a sampling frame. The research took place during a period of substantial reorganization of further education, and it could not always be established sufficiently early which colleges were teaching which courses. Restrictions deliberately imposed on the sampling frame were to delimit the population to colleges in England and Wales, because CSE is not normally taken outside these regions, and to exclude establishments (such as approved schools) that teach certain further education subjects, but which would not usually be regarded as part of the further education system.

13

After the pilot study described in the next paragraph it was decided not to draw a sample but to study the entire population described above. The chief reason for this was that far fewer students than expected were revealed by the pilot study to have taken CSE before beginning their further education courses. As it was desirable to investigate the predictive value of as many CSE subjects as possible, the optimum size of the sample approached the size of the population itself. Due to various factors the numbers included in the research fell short of the number in the population, but in the case of most courses included the majority.

Collection of the data

When the project began in May 1969 a sample of colleges were asked, at very short notice, to give details of students' CSE qualifications and performance in that summer's further education examinations. These data provided the basis of a pilot study, as a result of which alterations were made to the intended methods for collecting the data. The intention had been to ask colleges to supply all the necessary information, but for a variety of reasons this proved impracticable. The method eventually adopted was to request colleges to administer a questionnaire to students who had taken CSE at school and who were currently in the last year of one of the courses listed above. The questionnaire required students to give such information as the name of the school they had attended, and their own CSE results. Colleges that had agreed to participate in the project were sent questionnaires during the period January to March 1970. On the basis of these returns all the necessary data could be established. During July and August 1970 visits were made to the CSE examination boards where the self-reported grades were verified and any necessary alterations made. In September 1970 the further education examination results were obtained from City and Guilds and the Royal Society of Arts.

III. Results

1. Mechanical engineering technicians course, part I

Summary of results

The best predictors for this course (City and Guilds Subject 293) were physics and mathematics. Technical drawing also possessed predictive value, but the correlation with the further education results was not as strong. There was no evidence, however, that grades in any of these subjects could have been used to distinguish effectively between the students likely to pass and those likely to fail. Although each increase of a grade was associated with an increased chance of passing the further education examination, the lowest grades in these subjects nevertheless gave a better-than-even chance of passing. A similar situation obtained with the multiple predictors. Three combinations of CSE subjects predicted students' performance on the mechanical technicians course: mathematics with physics, English with technical drawing, and mathematics with technical drawing, the most efficient prediction being obtained from the first of these three pairs. Although a high proportion of the students in the trial group who were predicted to pass by the three combined predictors did so, a majority of those who were predicted to fail actually passed. Thus high grades in these CSE subjects indicated a good chance of success, but the lower grades gave little indication either way (Figs 1.1 and 1.2).

Analysis of the data

There were 906 students drawn from sixty-six colleges in the sample. Seventy-four per cent of these students passed the part I examination. Eight CSE subjects were considered as possible predictors of performance on this course: English, mathematics, technical drawing, physics, metalwork, geography, history, and general science. Six of the most commonly taken pairs of these subjects were studied as possible multiple predictors: English with mathematics, mathematics with technical drawing, technical drawing with physics, physics with metalwork, English with technical drawing, and mathematics with physics. The aim of the analysis was to test whether grades in these CSE subjects could discriminate between the students who would pass and those who would fail.

15

	Chances in 100 of	
Grade	←—Failing————————————————Passing→	Chances of Passing

PHYSICS

Grade		Chances of Passing
1		95
2		88
3		82
4		66
5 & U		61

MATHEMATICS

Grade		Chances of Passing
1		91
2		81
3		71
4		62
5 & U		54

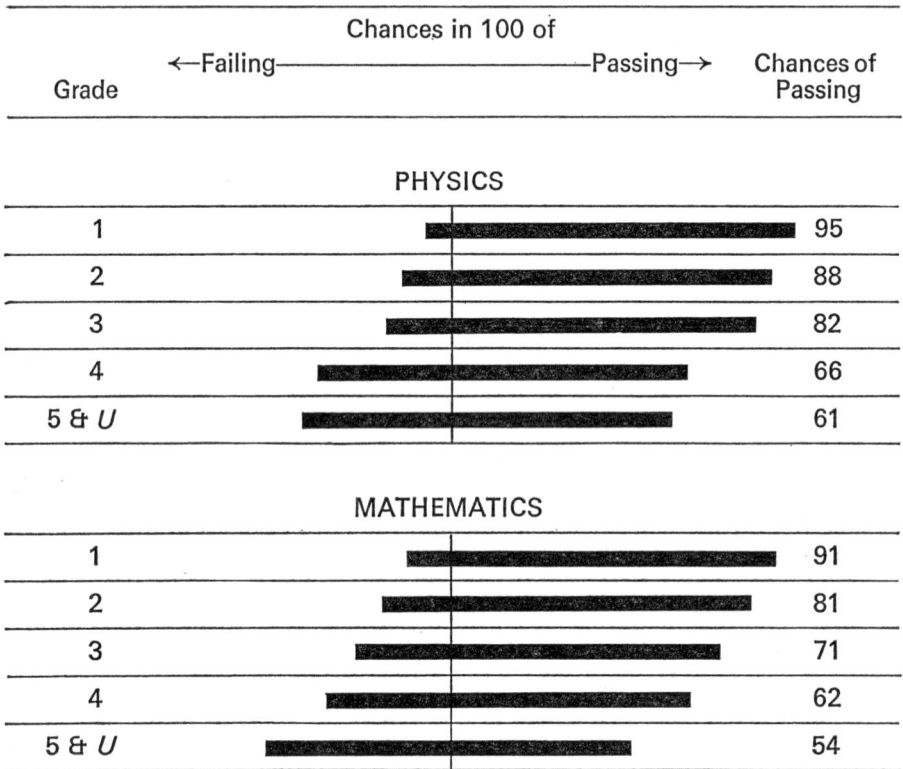

Fig. 1.1. Chances in 100 of passing the mechanical technicians course associated with each grade in CSE physics and mathematics.

Fig. 1.2. Proportions passing the mechanical technicians course with various combinations of CSE grades in physics and mathematics.

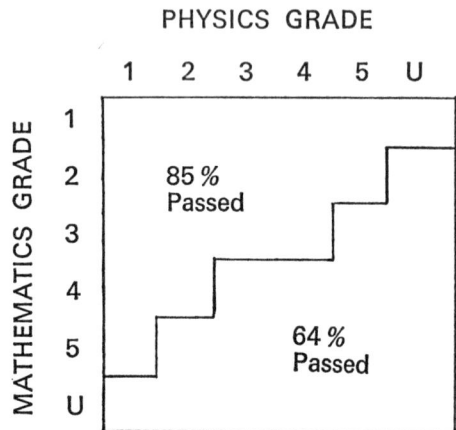

16

English as a predictor. There was no evidence to suggest that the students' performance in the City and Guilds examination was connected with their earlier performance in CSE English. Almost equal proportions of those with each grade passed.

Table 1.1 Performance of students with CSE English

Grade	1	2	3	4	5 & U	Total
Passed	40	112	166	162	50	530
Failed	12	39	67	59	28	205
Total	52	151	233	221	78	735
% in each grade who passed	77	74	71	73	64	

$C = .07$ $.50 > P > .30$

Mathematics as a predictor. Mathematics gave one of the best correlations with the mechanical technicians examination results.

Table 1.2 Performance of students with CSE mathematics

Grade	1	2	3	4	5 & U	Total
Passed	110	182	136	119	44	591
Failed	11	43	56	72	37	219
Total	121	225	192	191	81	810
% in each grade who passed	91	81	71	62	54	

$C = .25$ $.01 > P$

Each increase of a grade was associated with an increased chance of success in the part I examination, rising from a slightly better-than-even chance for those ungraded or awarded grade 5, to over ninety chances in a hundred for those with grade 1. Although low grades gave a poorer chance of passing than the higher grades, however, they gave no positive indication of failure. To learn which students were likely to fail, it would have been necessary to find a predictive measure other than CSE.

Technical drawing as a predictor. Technical drawing grades were significantly correlated with the further education results.

17

Table 1.3 Performance of students with CSE technical drawing

Grade	1	2	3	4	5 & U	Total
Passed	129	139	108	68	23	467
Failed	26	35	49	44	19	173
Total	155	174	157	112	42	640
% in each grade who passed	83	80	69	61	55	

$C = \cdot21$ $\qquad$ $\cdot01 > P$

Each increase of a grade was associated with an increased chance of passing the part I examination. As in the case of mathematics, however, students with the lowest grades had nevertheless a greater chance of passing than of failing.

Physics as a predictor. The best predictor among the CSE subjects investigated appears to have been physics. Its value in practice, however, would have been reduced by the fact that it was not one of the subjects most commonly taken by students on the mechanical technicians course (Appendix A, Table A. 1.1).

Table 1.4 Performance of students with CSE physics

Grade	1	2	3	4	5 & U	Total
Passed	35	81	89	81	28	314
Failed	2	11	19	42	18	92
Total	37	92	108	123	46	406
% in each grade who passed	95	88	82	66	61	

$C = \cdot27$ $\qquad$ $\cdot01 > P$

The implications of grades in physics were similar to the implications of grades in mathematics and technical drawing. A very strong expectation of success for those with grade 1 decreased to a better-than-even chance for those ungraded or awarded grade 5.

Metalwork as a predictor. The correlation between metalwork grades and the further education results, barely significant at the 5 per cent level, was slight. There was no evidence in the data collected that this subject would have had much predictive value.

18

Table 1.5 Performance of students with CSE metalwork

Grade	1	2	3	4	5 & U	Total
Passed	96	82	70	44	13	305
Failed	21	27	28	13	11	100
Total	117	109	98	57	24	405
% in each grade who passed	82	75	71	77	54	

$C = \cdot 15$ $\cdot 05 > P > \cdot 01$

Geography as a predictor. Students' geography grades were significantly correlated with their performance in the City and Guilds examination. Since, however, it is difficult to find a reason why geography should have been a valid predictor for this course, the case should be regarded as 'not proven'.

Table 1.6 Performance of students with CSE geography

Grade	1	2	3	4	5 & U	Total
Passed	48	85	75	77	20	305
Failed	7	19	37	31	15	109
Total	55	104	112	108	35	414
% in each grade who passed	87	82	67	71	57	

$C = \cdot 20$ $\cdot 01 > P$

History as a predictor. There was no evidence that history possessed predictive value.

Table 1.7 Performance of students with CSE history

Grade	1	2	3	4	5 & U	Total
Passed	18	41	58	54	20	191
Failed	4	10	15	23	13	65
Total	22	51	73	77	33	256
% in each grade who passed	82	80	80	70	61	

$C = \cdot 16$ $\cdot 20 > P > \cdot 10$

General science as a predictor. There was no evidence that general science grades could have been used to forecast students' performance in the mechanical technicians examination.

Table 1.8 Performance of students with CSE general science

Grade	1	2	3	4	5 & U	Total
Passed	17	42	36	33	9	137
Failed	6	12	18	12	10	58
Total	23	54	54	45	19	195
% in each grade who passed	74	78	67	73	47	

$C = \cdot19 \qquad \cdot20 > P > \cdot10$

Predicting college performance from combinations of CSE subjects. The sample was divided by random processes into a development group and a trial group of equal proportions. Discriminant functions were calculated for the six pairs of subjects to be investigated as possible multiple predictors, using the data of the development group. In two of the discriminant functions one of the combined subjects was assigned a small weight, and in these cases the discriminant function analysis was not pursued further.

Table 1.9 Discriminant functions for predicting performance on the mechanical technicians course

Combined Subjects	Weights	Mean D-scores Passed	Failed	Cut-off point
English and mathematics	0·042 0·550	*	*	*
Mathematics and tech. drawing	0·464 0·316	2·018	2·623	2·422
Tech. drawing and physics	0·258 0·549	2·190	2·838	2·656
Physics and metalwork	0·761 −0·038	*	*	*
English and tech. drawing	0·164 0·359	1·394	1·673	1·572
Mathematics and physics	0·589 0·385	2·648	3·588	3·344

* not calculated

The predictive validity of each of the four remaining discriminant functions was tested by applying it to the students in the trial group. The proportion of correct predictions each discriminant function made was compared with the proportion it would have made had it been predicting merely by a process of random classification. The significance of the improvement on random classification was then determined (Table 1.10). Three of the discriminant functions were found to be making genuine predictions.

Table 1.10 Validity of the discriminant functions for predicting performance on the mechanical technicians course

Combined subjects	Number of students in trial group	Proportion of results correctly predicted (%)
Mathematics and technical drawing	302	66**
Technical drawing and physics	162	62
English and technical drawing	278	64*
Mathematics and physics	195	71**

* an improvement over random classification at the 5 per cent level
** an improvement over random classification significant at the 1 per cent level

How efficient were these predictions? The best combination, mathematics and physics, correctly predicted the examination results of fewer than three-quarters of the students on whom it was tested. None of the three discriminant functions gave a clear discrimination between the students who passed and those who failed: in each case, a majority of those who were predicted to fail in fact passed (Table 1.11). Thus the combined CSE subjects failed to improve on the predictions obtained from the single predictors, neither method making it possible to identify the students who were likely to fail.

Conclusions

Evidence was found of a connexion between grades in a number of CSE subjects and performance in the mechanical technicians, part I, examination. In each case, however, high CSE grades were associated with success more strongly than low grades were with failure. Several reasons can be suggested for this. The most obvious is the high pass-rate in the mechanical technicians examination. It is

21

Table 1.11 Efficiency of the discriminant functions for predicting performance on the mechanical technicians course

	Mathematics and technical drawing		English and technical drawing		Mathematics and physics	
	Passed	*Failed*	*Passed*	*Failed*	*Passed*	*Failed*
Predicted to pass	164	31	151	36	117	20
Predicted to fail	73	34	63	28	37	21

possible, however, that the chances of success associated with the lower grades have been overestimated. One important factor here is that the students on whom the research was conducted had been selected by their employers for apprentice-ships, and those among them with the lower CSE grades would in all probability have been the most able of the whole population of school-leavers with such grades. The ways in which this factor affects the interpretation of the results described in this report are discussed at greater length in Chapter IV. A factor more specific to the sample under discussion is its heterogeneity (Appendix A, Table A.1.2). Fewer than half the students had begun this course in the aca-demic year immediately following the one in which they took CSE – in a few cases as many as three years had elapsed between obtaining a CSE certificate and commencing to study for the mechanical technicians, part I, examination. For the majority of the students in this position further periods of training had taken place in the intervening years, some of which, such as the G-course and mechanical craft practice, would have been of direct value as a preparation for the mechanical technicians course. It is doubtful, therefore, whether the CSE grades of many of the students in the sample accurately represented their attain-ment at the beginning of the course. It is likely in many cases that poor attain-ment at 16 had been remedied by the time that students began the mechanical technicians course, with the consequence that students with the lower grades performed better in the examination than they would have done had they begun this course immediately after school. For these reasons, it should not be inferred that CSE cannot be used to identify students likely to fail this course. The situa-tion is a complicated one, and more research in greater depth will be necessary before the full nature of the relationship between CSE grades and performance on this course is known.

2. Electrical technicians course, part I

Summary of results

Physics and mathematics were the best single-subject predictors of students' performance on this course (City and Guilds Subject 57). Combined grades in mathematics and physics gave the best multiple prediction, followed by combined grades in English and mathematics (Figs 2.1 and 2.2).

Analysis of the data

The sample of students following the electrical technicians course comprised 362 students in forty-nine colleges. The majority were attending college on a day-release basis, although small numbers of block-release and full-time students were also included. Their ages ranged from 17 to 21, some having begun the college course soon after leaving school, others having taken CSE and left school two or three years before attending college. The sample thus showed the heterogeneity of age, background, and mode of study typical of further education. Sixty-three per cent of these students passed the part I examination. The aim of the analysis was to test whether CSE results could have been used to distinguish those who would pass from those who would fail.

Nine CSE subjects were investigated as possible predictors of performance on this course: English, mathematics, technical drawing, physics, metalwork, woodwork, geography, history, and general science. Two of the most commonly-taken pairs of subjects were investigated as possible multiple predictors: English combined with mathematics and mathematics combined with physics.

English as a predictor. There was no evidence that English grades could have been used to predict the performance of the students in the sample.

Table 2.1 Performance of students with CSE English

Grade	1	2	3	4	5 & U	Total
Passed	11	35	66	57	16	185
Failed	3	23	36	41	13	116
Total	14	58	102	98	29	301
% in each grade who passed	79	60	65	58	55	

$C = \cdot10$ $\qquad \cdot70 > P > \cdot50$

23

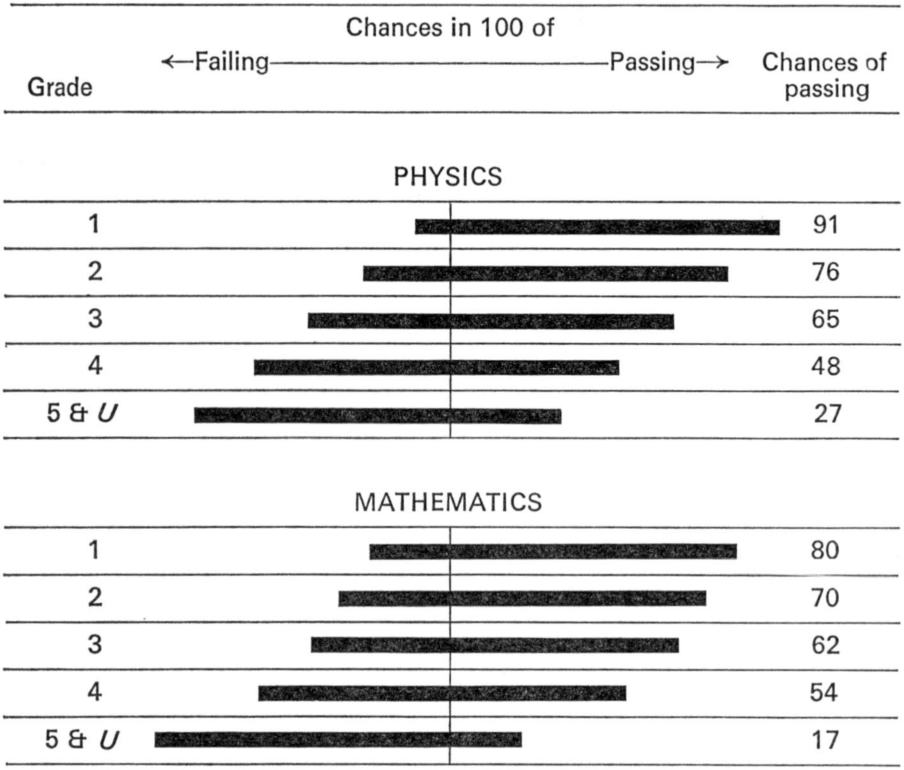

Grade	←Failing —————————————————— Passing→	Chances of passing

PHYSICS

Grade		Chances of passing
1		91
2		76
3		65
4		48
5 & *U*		27

MATHEMATICS

Grade		Chances of passing
1		80
2		70
3		62
4		54
5 & *U*		17

Fig. 2.1. Chances in 100 of passing the electrical technicians course associated with each grade in physics and mathematics.

Fig. 2.2. Proportions passing the electrical technicians course with various combinations of CSE grades in mathematics and physics, and in English and mathematics.

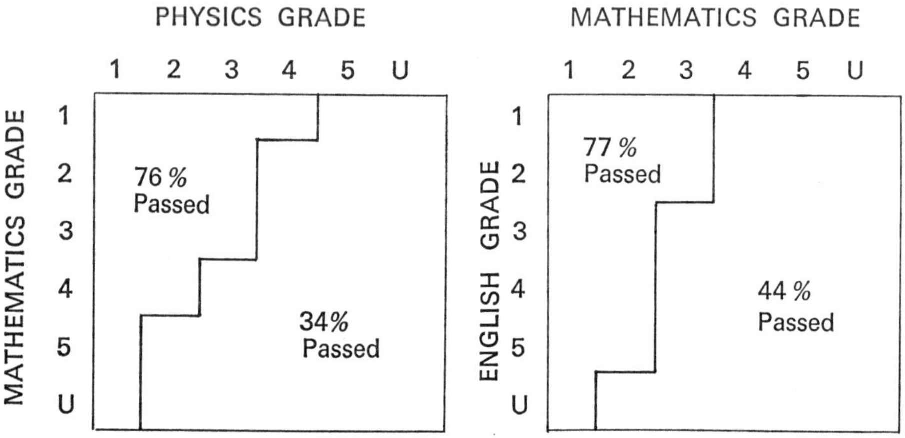

PHYSICS GRADE   MATHEMATICS GRADE

76 % Passed

34% Passed

77 % Passed

44 % Passed

Mathematics as a predictor. Mathematics grades were significantly correlated with the further education results.

Table 2.2 Performance of students with CSE mathematics

Grade	1	2	3	4	5 & U	Total
Passed	32	64	51	36	5	188
Failed	8	27	31	31	24	121
Total	40	91	82	67	29	309
% in each grade who passed	80	70	62	54	17	

$C = \cdot 33$ \qquad $\cdot 01 > P$

Students ungraded or awarded grade 5 had a very poor chance of passing the electrical technicians examination (only 17 chances in 100). Those with grade 4 and above were more likely to pass than fail, the expectation of success rising steadily with each increase of a CSE grade. If students with grade 4 and above had been predicted to pass, and those with grade 5 and below predicted to fail, 70 per cent of the predictions would have been correct.

Technical drawing as a predictor. There was no evidence that technical drawing grades could have been used to distinguish those who would pass the electrical technicians examination from those who would fail. A greater proportion of the students with grade 5 or below passed than with grade 2.

Table 2.3 Performance of students with CSE technical drawing

Grade	1	2	3	4	5 & U	Total
Passed	38	32	28	24	14	136
Failed	14	23	31	15	6	89
Total	52	55	59	39	20	225
% in each grade who passed	73	60	48	62	70	

$C = \cdot 20$ \qquad $\cdot 10 > P > \cdot 05$

Physics as a predictor. Physics proved to be one of the best predictors. A highly significant correlation between physics grades and the electrical technicians results is revealed by the data in Table 2.4.

Table 2.4 Performance of students with CSE physics

Grade	1	2	3	4	5 & U	Total
Passed	20	42	42	30	4	138
Failed	2	13	23	33	11	82
Total	22	55	65	63	15	220
% in each grade who passed	91	76	65	48	27	

$C = \cdot 35$ $\cdot 01 > P$

Each increase of a CSE grade was accompanied by an increase in the probability of success. Students ungraded or obtaining grade 5 were more likely to fail than pass (27 chances in 100 of passing). Grade 4 gave no clear indication either way, and grades 3 and above indicated a likelihood of success. If physics grades had been interpreted in this way, the further education results of 48 per cent of these students would have been predicted correctly, with 30 per cent in the 'don't know' category.

Metalwork as a predictor. There was no evidence that metalwork possessed predictive value.

Table 2.5 Performance of students with CSE metalwork

Grade	1	2	3	4	5 & U	Total
Passed	17	18	18	13	5	71
Failed	7	15	17	15	4	58
Total	24	33	35	28	9	129
% in each grade who passed	71	55	51	46	56	

$C = \cdot 16$ $\cdot 50 > P > \cdot 30$

Woodwork as a predictor. No significant correlation was evident between wood-work grades and performance on the electrical technicians course.

Table 2.6 Performance of students with CSE woodwork

Grade	1	2	3	4	5 & U	Total
Passed	10	15	20	11	3	59
Failed	2	7	7	7	6	29
Total	12	22	27	18	9	88
% in each grade who passed	83	68	74	61	33	

$C = \cdot28 \qquad \cdot20 > P > \cdot10$

Geography as a predictor. Geography grades were significantly correlated with the electrical technicians examination results. However, the relationship was uneven, slightly more of the students with grade 4 passing than with grade 3. It is difficult to explain why grades in this subject should be related to performance in the electrical technicians examination. There is a possibility that when treated as a science subject, CSE geography grades reflect the presence or otherwise of abilities which also determine engineering attainment. However, without con-crete information about the abilities measured by both examinations, such con-jectures cannot carry much weight, and so the results given here should be treated with caution.

Table 2.7 Performance of students with CSE geography

Grade	1	2	3	4	5 & U	Total
Passed	22	35	28	25	5	115
Failed	4	13	21	16	15	69
Total	26	48	49	41	20	184
% in each grade who passed	85	71	57	61	25	

$C = \cdot33 \qquad \cdot01 > P$

27

History as a predictor. History showed no signs of predictive value.

Table 2.8 Performance of students with CSE history

Grade	1	2	3	4	5 & U	Total
Passed	8	14	15	13	13	63
Failed	4	5	10	15	8	42
Total	12	19	25	28	21	105
% in each grade who passed	67	74	60	47	62	

$C = \cdot19 \qquad \cdot50 > P > \cdot30$

General science as a predictor. The apparent correlation between general science grades and the further education results was due mainly to the high probability of success associated with grade 1, there being no evidence of a correlation between further education performance and the lower grades. It is conceivable that the grade 1 successes are a chance effect, and so the predictive value of general science should be regarded as 'not proven'.

Table 2.9 Performance of students with CSE general science

Grade	1	2	3	4	5 & U		Total
Passed	10	9	7	5	(7)	2	33
Failed	1	8	11	6	(8)	2	28
Total	11	17	18		15		61
% in each grade who passed	91	53	39		47		

$C = \cdot36 \qquad \cdot05 > P > \cdot025$

Predicting performance on the electrical technicians course from combined pairs of CSE subjects. The sample was divided by random processes into a development group and a trial group, the former comprising two-thirds of the students. Using the data of the development group, discriminant functions were calculated for the two pairs of subjects to be investigated as possible multiple predictors (Table 2.10).

28

Table 2.10 Discriminant functions for predicting performance on the electrical technicians course

Combined subjects	Weights	Mean D-scores Passed	Mean D-scores Failed	Cut-off point
Mathematics and physics	0·408 0·678	2·792	3·739	3·332
English and mathematics	0·171 0·438	1·679	2·011	1·812

The predictive validity of the discriminant functions was tested by applying them to the students in the trial group. The proportion of correct predictions made by each discriminant function was compared with the proportion it would have made had it been predicting merely by random classification. The significance of the improvement on random classification was then determined (Table 2.11).

Table 2.11 Validity of the discriminant functions for predicting performance on the electrical technicians course

Combined subjects	Number of students in trial group	Proportion of results correctly predicted by the discriminant function (%)
Mathematics and physics	70	71**
English and mathematics	98	66**

** an improvement on random classification significant at the 1 per cent level

Both combinations of subjects proved to have been making fairly efficient predictions (Table 2.12). Seventy-six per cent of those predicted to pass by the discriminant function for mathematics and physics did so, and 66 per cent of those predicted to fail did so. The corresponding figures for the combination of English and mathematics were 77 per cent and 56 per cent respectively. Thus the combination of mathematics and physics would appear to have been the better predictor, having given a more accurate indication of which students were likely to fail.

Table 2.12 Efficiency of the discriminant functions for predicting performance on the electrical technicians course

	Mathematics and physics		English and mathematics	
	Passed	*Failed*	*Passed*	*Failed*
Predicted to pass	31	10	37	11
Predicted to fail	10	19	22	28

3. General course in engineering

Summary of results

The best single-subject predictors of whether students would qualify for entry to ONC* at the end of the G-course (City and Guilds Subject 287) were mathematics and physics. English and technical drawing also possessed predictive validity, but the correlations between grades in these subjects and performance on the G-course were lower. Valid predictions were also obtained from several pairs of combined CSE subjects, the two most efficient being mathematics combined with physics and English combined with mathematics. The probability of success associated with grades in the subjects with predictive validity is given in Figures 3.1 and 3.2. In general, low grades implied a poor chance of qualifying for entry to ONC, while good grades gave little indication either way.

Analysis of the data

The sample comprised 445 students in thirty-five colleges of further education. About two-thirds were on day-release, the others studying either full-time or by block-release. Thirty-two per cent of the students qualified for entry to an ONC course, and a further 42 per cent obtained credits in two of the four papers, which in most colleges would be considered sufficient for entry to the second year of a technician course. In all, 74 per cent qualified for a course more advanced than a craft course. The object of the investigation was to test whether, by referring to their CSE grades, those who would qualify for entry to ONC could be distinguished from those who would fail to do so. Nine CSE subjects were studied as possible predictors: English, mathematics, technical drawing, physics, metalwork, woodwork, geography, history, and general science. Five pairs of these subjects were studied as possible multiple predictors: English with mathematics,

* A student qualifying for entry to an ONC course would also qualify for entry to an OND course.

Grade		Chances of qualifying

MATHEMATICS

Grade		Chances of qualifying
1		54
2		29
3		20
4		12
5 & *U*		5

PHYSICS

Grade		Chances of qualifying
1		44
2		39
3		33
4		14
5 & *U*		13

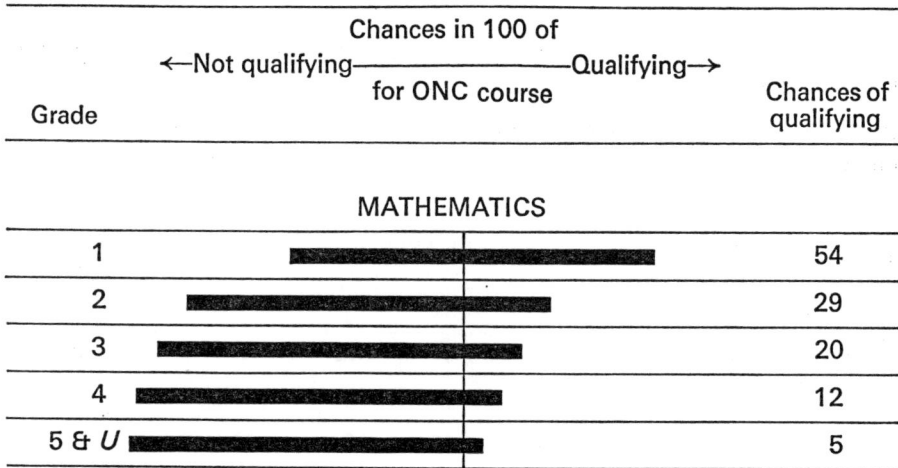

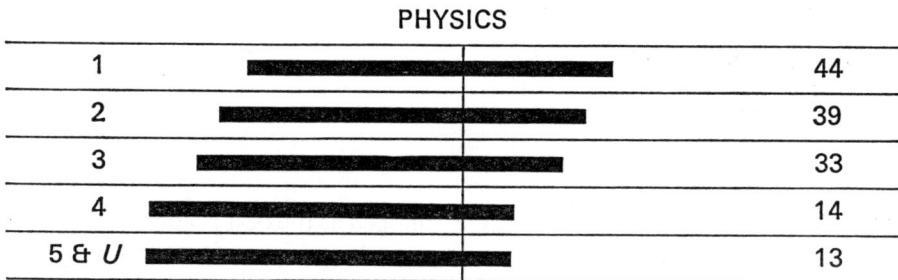

Fig. 3.1. Chances in 100 of qualifying for ONC associated with each grade in CSE mathematics and physics.

Fig. 3.2. Proportions qualifying for ONC with various combinations of CSE grades in mathematics and physics and in English and mathematics.

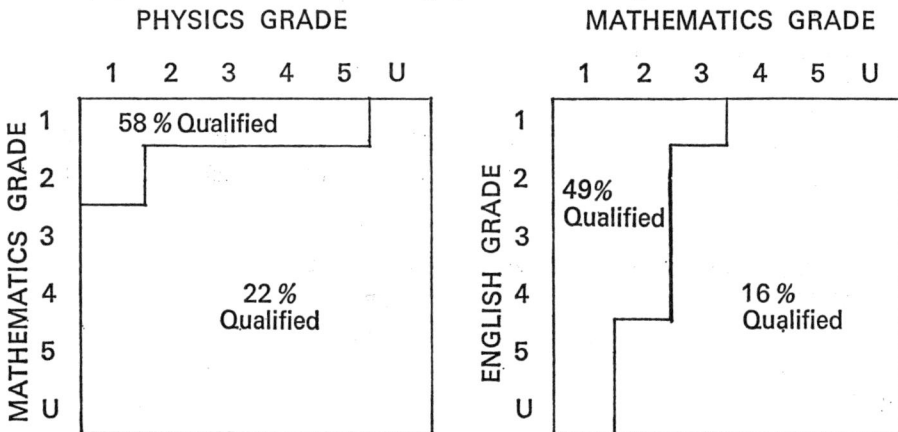

PHYSICS GRADE

MATHEMATICS GRADE

English with technical drawing, mathematics with technical drawing, mathematics with physics, and technical drawing with physics.

English as a predictor. The correlation between English grades and performance on the G-course, although significant at the 5 per cent level, was low.

Table 3.1 Performance of students with CSE English

Grade	1	2	3	4	5 & U	Total
Qualified for entry to ONC course	12	38	34	22	3	109
Did not qualify	18	60	77	70	22	247
Total	30	98	111	92	25	356
% in each grade qualifying for entry to ONC course	40	39	31	24	12	

$C = ·17$ $·05 > P > ·01$

Mathematics as a predictor. Mathematics emerged as the best predictor. Students with grade 1 had a better-than-even chance of qualifying for entry to ONC, but with each decrease of a grade, the chances of success fell substantially.

Table 3.2 Performance of students with CSE mathematics

Grade	1	2	3	4	5 & U	Total
Qualified for entry to ONC course	56	29	17	7	1	110
Did not qualify	47	70	68	54	19	258
Total	103	99	85	61	20	368
% in each grade qualifying for entry to ONC course	54	29	20	12	5	

$C = ·37$ $·01 > P$

Technical drawing as a predictor. Technical drawing grades were significantly correlated with the G-course results, but the correlation was weak. There was little difference in the expectation of success associated with grades 2, 3, and 4.

Table 3.3 Performance of students with CSE technical drawing

Grade	1	2	3	4	5 & U	Total
Qualified for entry to ONC course	36	19	19	12	0	86
Did not qualify	55	46	43	30	16	190
Total	91	65	62	42	16	276
% in each grade qualifying for entry to ONC course	40	29	31	29	0	

$C = \cdot 19 \qquad \cdot 05 > P > \cdot 01$

Physics as a predictor. Physics was one of the best predictors for this course, giving the second-highest correlation with the G-course results.

Table 3.4 Performance of students with CSE physics

Grade	1	2	3	4	5 & U	Total
Qualified for entry to ONC course	12	37	22	7	2	80
Did not qualify	15	57	45	42	14	173
Total	27	94	67	49	16	253
% in each grade qualifying for entry to ONC course	44	39	33	14	13	

$C = \cdot 24 \qquad \cdot 01 > P$

33

Metalwork as a predictor. Metalwork showed no evidence of possessing predictive value.

Table 3.5 Performance of students with CSE metalwork

Grade	1	2	3	4		5 & U	Total
Qualified for entry to ONC course	22	9	7	7	(11)	4	49
Did not qualify	37	22	26	17	(20)	3	105
Total	59	31	33		31		154
% in each grade qualifying for entry to ONC course	37	29	21		35		

$C = \cdot 14 \qquad \cdot 50 > P > \cdot 30$

Woodwork as a predictor. There was no evidence that woodwork grades could have been used to predict performance on the G-course.

Table 3.6 Performance of students with CSE woodwork

Grade	1	2	3	4		5 & U	Total
Qualified for entry to ONC course	15	5	5	3	(3)	0	28
Did not qualify	27	25	19	13	(16)	3	87
Total	42	30	24		19		115
% in each grade qualifying for entry to ONC course	36	17	21		16		

$C = \cdot 20 \qquad \cdot 20 > P > \cdot 10$

Geography as a predictor. There was no evidence that geography possessed predictive value.

Table 3.7 Performance of students with CSE geography

Grade	1	2	3	4	5 & U	Total
Qualified for entry to ONC course	21	23	15	9	3	71
Did not qualify	23	44	33	36	10	146
Total	44	67	48	45	13	217
% in each grade qualifying for entry to ONC course	48	34	31	20	23	

$C = \cdot20$ $\quad \cdot10 > P > \cdot05$

History as a predictor. History showed no evidence of possessing predictive value.

Table 3.8 Performance of students with CSE history

Grade	1	2	3	4	5 & U	Total
Qualified for entry to ONC course	10	10	15	9	4	48
Did not qualify	13	18	26	22	11	90
Total	23	28	41	31	15	138
% in each grade qualifying for entry to ONC course	44	36	37	29	27	

$C = \cdot11$ $\quad \cdot90 > P > \cdot75$

General science as a predictor. The apparent correlation between general science grades and performance on the G-course was not significant.

Table 3.9 Performance of students with CSE general science

Grade	1	2	3	4	5 & U		Total
Qualified for entry to ONC course	11	6	4	1	(1)	0	22
Did not qualify	9	15	13	7	(8)	1	45
Total	20	21	17	9			67
% in each grade qualifying for entry to ONC course	55	29	24	11			

$C = \cdot33$ $\cdot10 > P > \cdot05$

Predicting performance on the G-course from combined pairs of CSE subjects. The sample was divided by random processes into a development group and a trial group of equal proportions. Using the data in the development group, discriminant functions were calculated for the five pairs of CSE subjects to be investi-

Table 3.10 Discriminant functions for predicting performance on the G-course

Combined subjects	Weights	Mean D-scores		Cut-off point
		Qualified for entry to ONC	Did not qualify for entry to ONC	
English and mathematics	0·240 0·567	1·691	2·263	2·151
English and tech. drawing	0·303 0·286	1·422	1·627	1·490
Mathematics and tech. drawing	0·582 0·097	*	*	*
Mathematics and physics	0·468 0·147	1·248	1·610	1·369
Tech. drawing and physics	0·238 0·205	1·032	1·181	1·069

* not calculated

gated as possible multiple predictors (Table 3.10). In one of these, one of the combined subjects was assigned a small weight, and in this case the analysis was not taken further.

The validity of the discriminant functions was tested by applying them to the students in the trial group (Table 3.11). First, it was found how many of the students' results would have been correctly predicted if the discriminant functions had been predicting merely by a process of random selection. Then the proportion of the students in the trial group whose results were correctly predicted was compared with this, and the significance of the improvement determined. All four discriminant functions were found to be making genuine predictions.

Table 3.11 Validity of the discriminant functions for predicting performance on the G-course

Combined subjects	Number of students in the trial group	Proportion of results correctly predicted (%)
English and mathematics	159	66**
English and technical drawing	129	62*
Mathematics and physics	105	71**
Technical drawing and physics	82	64*

* an improvement on random selection significant at the 5 per cent level
** an improvement on random selection significant at the 1 per cent level

By the criterion of the number of correct predictions, the most efficient predictor was mathematics combined with physics, followed by mathematics combined with English. All four discriminant functions, however, were less reliable in indicating which students would qualify for entry to ONC than in indicating which students would fail to qualify. In each case only about half of those predicted to qualify did so, whereas the results of about 80 per cent of those predicted not to qualify were predicted correctly (Table 3.12).

Table 3.12 Efficiency of the discriminant functions for predicting performance on the G-course

	Mathematics and physics		English and mathematics	
	Qualified	Did not qualify	Qualified	Did not qualify
Predicted to qualify for ONC	19	14	41	42
Predicted not to qualify for ONC	16	56	12	64

	Technical drawing and physics		English and technical drawing	
	Qualified	Did not qualify	Qualified	Did not qualify
Predicted to qualify for ONC	18	18	26	31
Predicted not to qualify for ONC	11	35	18	54

An effect similar to this was observed with the single-subject predictors. A possible explanation is that the ability and attainment measured by CSE were a necessary but not sufficient requirement for success on the G-course.

4. Basic engineering craft studies course (mechanical bias)

Summary of results

The best single-subject predictors of this course (City and Guilds Subject 500) were metalwork and woodwork. The best multiple predictors among those studied were metalwork combined with physics and metalwork combined with technical drawing. In no case, however, was it possible to identify which students were unlikely to obtain credits – even candidates with the lower grades in these subjects had a better chance of passing with credit than of not doing so.

38

Chances in 100 of a result
←—Below credit———————————Credit or above—→
Grade
Chances
of credit
or above

METALWORK

Grade	Chances of credit or above
1	99
2	88
3	84
4	61
5 & *U*	47

WOODWORK

Grade	Chances of credit or above
1	98
2	95
3	73
4	65
5 & *U*	50

Fig. 4.1. Chances in 100 of passing with credit on the basic craft studies course associated with each grade in metalwork and woodwork.

Fig. 4.2. Proportions passing with credit on the basic craft studies course with various combinations of CSE grades in metalwork and physics, and in metalwork and technical drawing.

METALWORK GRADE

1 2 3 4 5 U

PHYSICS GRADE

1
2
3
4
5
U

92 %
Passed
with credit

52 %
Passed
with credit

METALWORK GRADE

1 2 3 4 5 U

TECHNICAL DRAWING GRADE

1
2
3
4
5
U

92 %
Passed
with credit

60 %
Passed
with credit

Analysis of the data

The sample comprised 1050 students in fifty-one colleges of further education. The majority were studying by day-release, but the sample also included substantial numbers of full-time students and a few block-release students. (Appendix A, Table A.4.2). Almost all had taken CSE in 1969, beginning the craft studies course in September of that year. The pass-rate in the sample was 97 per cent, with 82 per cent passing with credit and 7 per cent passing with distinction. For the reasons given in Chapter II it was decided to investigate whether CSE grades could have been used to predict which students would pass with credit or distinction. Nine subjects were studied as possible predictors: English, mathematics, technical drawing, physics, metalwork, woodwork, geography, history, and general science. Seven commonly-taken pairs of these subjects were investigated as possible multiple predictors: English with mathematics, mathematics with technical drawing, technical drawing with physics, physics with metalwork, English with technical drawing, mathematics with physics, and technical drawing with metalwork.

Metalwork and woodwork as predictors. These two subjects proved to be the best single predictors of performance on the craft studies course. In both subjects, students ungraded or awarded grade 5 had an even chance of obtaining a credit or distinction. Each increase of a grade was associated with an increased expectation of reaching this standard, the students with grade 1 having had an almost certain expectation of doing so.

Table 4.1 Performance of students with CSE metalwork

Grade	1	2	3	4	5 & U	Total
Credit or above	119	114	108	54	15	410
Below credit	1	15	21	34	17	88
Total	120	129	129	88	32	498
% in each grade with credit or above	99	88	84	61	47	

$C = \cdot 40$ $\cdot 01 > P$

Table 4.2 Performance of students with CSE woodwork

Grade	1	2	3	4	5 & U	Total
Credit or above	44	72	66	32	8	222
Below credit	1	4	25	17	8	55
Total	45	76	91	49	16	277
% in each grade with credit or above	98	95	73	65	50	

$C = \cdot 37$ $\quad\quad \cdot 01 > P$

Mathematics, technical drawing, physics, geography, history, and general science as predictors. Grades in all these subjects were found to be significantly correlated with the craft studies results, but the correlations were lower than those obtained from metalwork and woodwork.

Table 4.3 Performance of students with CSE mathematics

Grade	1	2	3	4	5 & U	Total
Credit or above	59	114	177	213	160	723
Below credit	1	7	18	45	86	157
Total	60	121	195	258	246	880
% in each grade with credit or above	98	94	91	83	65	

$C = \cdot 31$ $\quad\quad \cdot 01 > P$

Table 4.4 Performance of students with CSE technical drawing

Grade	1	2	3	4	5 & U	Total
Credit or above	102	128	144	130	89	593
Below credit	1	11	20	30	46	108
Total	103	139	164	160	135	701
% in each grade with credit or above	99	92	88	81	66	

$C = \cdot 30$ $\cdot 01 > P$

Table 4.5 Performance of students with CSE physics

Grade	1	2	3	4	5 & U	Total
Credit or above	11	79	121	157	85	453
Below credit	0	0	8	26	35	69
Total	11	79	129	183	120	522
% in each grade with credit or above	100	100	94	86	71	

$C = \cdot 30$ $\cdot 01 > P$

Table 4.6 Performance of students with CSE geography

Grade	1	2	3	4	5 & U	Total
Credit or above	34	89	117	109	66	415
Below credit	0	9	22	40	37	108
Total	34	98	139	149	103	523
% in each grade with credit or above	100	91	84	73	64	

$C = \cdot27$ $\cdot01 > P$

Table 4.7 Performance of students with CSE history

Grade	1	2	3	4	5 & U	Total
Credit or above	24	34	59	96	55	268
Below credit	2	5	17	29	35	88
Total	26	39	76	125	90	356
% in each grade with credit or above	92	87	78	77	61	

$C = \cdot22$ $\cdot01 > P$

Table 4.8 Performance of students with CSE general science

Grade	1	2	3	4	5 & U	Total
Credit or above	16	38	43	47	22	166
Below credit	0	1	6	12	14	33
Total	16	39	49	59	36	199
% in each grade with credit or above	100	97	88	80	61	

$C = \cdot34$ $\cdot01 > P$

English as a predictor. English grades gave the lowest correlation with the craft studies results.

Table 4.9 Performance of students with CSE English

Grade	1	2	3	4	5 & U	Total
Credit or above	29	113	183	274	122	721
Below credit	0	13	51	62	47	173
Total	29	126	234	336	169	894
% in each grade with credit or above	100	90	78	82	72	

$C = \cdot16$ $\cdot01 > P$

Predicting performance on the craft studies course from combined grades in pairs of CSE subjects. The sample was divided by random processes into a development group and a trial group of equal numbers. Discriminant functions were calculated for the seven pairs of subjects to be studied as possible multiple predictors, using the data of the development group. In one case the weight assigned to one of the combined subjects was small, and for this combination the discriminant function analysis was not pursued further.

Table 4.10 Discriminant functions for predicting performance on the craft studies course

Combined subjects	Weights	Mean D-scores		Cut-off point
		Credit or above	Below credit	
English and mathematics	−0·004 0·626	*	*	*
Mathematics and technical drawing	0·385 0·416	2·570	3·319	3·195
Technical drawing and physics	0·404 0·533	3·103	3·983	3·985
Physics and metalwork	0·325 1·005	3·495	4·149	4·056
English and technical drawing	0·163 0·519	2·142	2·713	2·618
Mathematics and physics	0·244 0·787	3·578	4·600	4·472
Technical drawing and metalwork	0·383 0·800	2·991	4·549	3·327

* not calculated

In order to test whether they were valid predictors the discriminant functions were applied to the students in the trial group. The proportion of correct predictions obtained from each discriminant function was compared with the proportion which would have been obtained if the discriminant function had been predicting merely by a process of random selection. A test of the significance of the improvement on random selection was then applied. All six discriminant functions proved to have been making genuine predictions.

Table 4.11 Validity of the discriminant functions for predicting performance on the craft studies course

Combined subjects	Number of students in the trial group	Proportion of these students whose results were correctly predicted (%)
Mathematics and technical drawing	284	70**
Technical drawing and physics	174	80**
Physics and metalwork	138	83**
English and technical drawing	306	69**
Mathematics and physics	226	77**
Technical drawing and metalwork	195	81**

** an improvement on random selection significant at the 1 per cent level

Using as a criterion the number of correct predictions they gave, a comparison of the efficiency of the six discriminant functions suggested that the best was metalwork combined with physics, followed by metalwork combined with technical drawing. Table 4.12 shows the predictions made by the discriminant functions in greater detail. It can be seen that although the best multiple predictor (metalwork and physics) was correct in 83 per cent of its predictions, it was unreliable in predicting which students would fail to reach the credit standard in the examination. Fifty-two per cent of the students it predicted not to obtain credits in fact did so. A similar situation was true in the case of the other multiple predictors, and thus they failed to improve on the quality of prediction given by the single-subject predictors. It was possible to say of a student with high grades that he possessed a strong chance of passing the craft studies course with credit or distinction, but it was not possible to say that a student with low grades had a poor chance of reaching this level.

Table 4.12 Efficiency of the predictions obtained from the discriminant functions

	Physics and metalwork		Technical drawing and metalwork		Technical drawing and physics	
	Credit or above	Below credit	Credit or above	Below credit	Credit or above	Below credit
Predicted to obtain credits	100	9	140	13	127	9
Predicted not to obtain credits	15	14	25	17	25	13

	Mathematics and physics		Mathematics and technical drawing		English and technical drawing	
	Credit or above	Below credit	Credit or above	Below credit	Credit or above	Below credit
Predicted to obtain credits	154	14	168	14	179	18
Predicted not to obtain credits	37	21	71	31	77	32

5. General catering course

Summary of results

The most efficient predictors of performance on this course (City and Guilds Subject 441) were general science and English. Of the ten subjects investigated, domestic science, biology, geography, and history also showed signs of predictive validity, but the correlations obtained for these subjects were weaker. A combination of geography and domestic science also provided valid predictions, but the number of students on whom it was tested was small and so its value should be accepted with caution.

Analysis of the data

The sample comprised 369 full-time students in twenty-seven colleges. Most had taken CSE in 1969, entering college in September of that year. Eighty-six per cent passed the examination at the end of the course, 44 per cent with credit. The high pass-rate suggested that there would have been little point in using CSE to predict whether or not a student was likely to pass. For the purposes of the research, therefore, students were classified into two categories: 'passed at the credit level' and 'did not attain the credit level'. The reasons for adopting this procedure are explained more fully in Chapter II.

English as a predictor. English grades gave one of the best indications of which students were likely to reach the credit standard.

Table 5.1 Performance of students with CSE English

Grade	1	2	3	4	5 & U	Total
Credit	15	43	40	28	3	129
Below credit	5	32	44	70	29	180
Total	20	75	84	98	32	309
% in each grade with credit	75	57	48	29	9	

$C = \cdot 35$ $\qquad \cdot 01 > P$

Students with grade 1 in English had a strong expectation of passing the catering examination with credit. There was no clear indication either way for those with grades 2 and 3, and those with grade 4 or below had a relatively poor chance of obtaining credits. If English grades had been interpreted in this way, the further

48

Grade	Chances in 100 of a result ←Below credit————————Credit or above→	Chances of credit or above
GENERAL SCIENCE		
1, 2,3		71
4, 5, *U*		22
ENGLISH		
1		75
2		57
3		48
4		29
5 & *U*		9

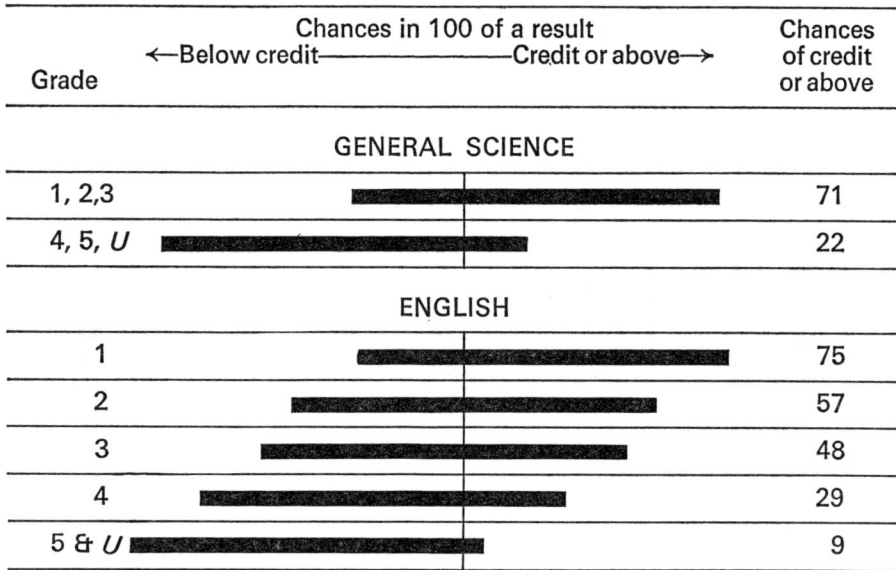

Fig. 5.1. Chances in 100 of passing with credit on the general catering course associated with each grade in general science and English.

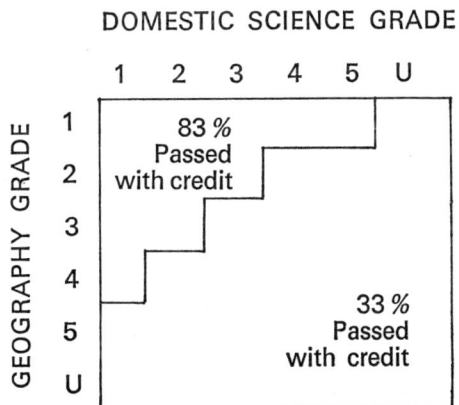

Fig. 5.2. Proportions passing with credit on the general catering course with various combinations of CSE grades in geography and domestic science.

DOMESTIC SCIENCE GRADE

GEOGRAPHY GRADE

83 % Passed with credit

33 % Passed with credit

education results of 37 per cent of these students would have been predicted correctly, with 51 per cent in the 'don't know' category.

Mathematics as a predictor. Mathematics showed little evidence of predictive value.

Table 5.2 Performance of students with CSE mathematics

Grade	1	2	3	4	5 & U	Total
Credit	3 (20)	17	24	38	26	108
Below credit	5 (17)	12	25	50	55	147
Total	37		49	88	81	255
% in each grade with credit	54		49	43	32	

$C = \cdot16$ $\cdot10 > P > \cdot05$

History as a predictor. Grades in history were found to be significantly correlated with the catering results, but the relationship was irregular. It can be seen from Table 5.3 that there was little difference between the expectation of success associated with grade 1 and that associated with grade 2, and that a similar situation existed between grade 4 and the grades below. Thus although students' performance in the catering examination was connected with their earlier performance in CSE history, differences of a grade do not appear to have been of much predictive significance.

Table 5.3 Performance of students with CSE history

Grade	1	2	3	4	5 & U	Total
Credit	7	13	18	12	9	59
Below credit	5	9	20	36	22	92
Total	12	22	38	48	31	151
% in each grade with credit	58	59	47	25	29	

$C = \cdot28$ $\cdot05 > P > \cdot01$

Geography as a predictor. Geography gave one of the strongest correlations with performance in the catering examination. This result is difficult to interpret, as there was no common content between geography syllabuses and the general

50

catering course syllabus. It is conceivable that geography gradings measured the strength of some aptitude necessary for outstanding performance in catering, but without further research the case for its predictive value should be taken as 'not proven'.

Table 5.4 Performance of students with CSE geography

Grade	1	2	3	4	5 & U	Total
Credit	12	17	22	17	4	72
Below credit	4	15	29	28	22	98
Total	16	32	51	45	26	170
% in each grade with credit	75	53	43	38	15	

$C = \cdot31$ $\cdot01 > P$

Domestic science as a predictor. There was a significant correlation between students' domestic science grades and their performance on the general catering course. However, as the data of Table 5.5 show, the relationship between the two variables was irregular. There was little difference between the expectation of success associated with grade 3 and that associated with grades 4 and below, and students with grade 2 appear to have had a slightly better chance of obtaining credits than those with grade 1. In the data collected, differences of one grade were not always of predictive significance. Students with grade 2 or above possessed a strong expectation of obtaining a credit; those with grade 3 or below a relatively poor chance. If those with grade 2 or above had been predicted to pass with credit, and the others predicted not to, 65 per cent of the predictions would have been correct.

Table 5.5 Performance of students with CSE domestic science

Grade	1	2	3	4	5 & U		Total
Credit	22	30	14	(9)	10	(1)	76
Below credit	14	15	26	(16)	19	(3)	74
Total	36	45	40		29		150
% in each grade with credit	61	67	35		34		

$C = \cdot30$ $\cdot01 > P$

Foreign languages as predictors. French, German, and Spanish were included under this heading. There was no evidence that these subjects possessed predictive value.

Table 5.6 Performance of students with CSE in a foreign language

Grade	1		2	3	4	5 & U	Total
Credit	2	(10)	8	7	8	7	32
Below credit	3	(5)	2	9	9	8	31
Total		15		16	17	15	63
% in each grade with credit		67		44	47	47	

$C = \cdot 18$ $\cdot 75 > P > \cdot 50$

Needlework as a predictor. There was no evidence that needlework grades could have been used to predict the further education results of these students.

Table 5.7 Performance of students with CSE needlework

Grade	1	2	3	4	5 & U		Total
Credit	7	8	12	5	(8)	3	35
Below credit	3	5	10	6	(9)	3	27
Total	10	13	22		17		62
% in each grade with credit	70	62	55		47		

$C = \cdot 16$ $\cdot 75 > P > \cdot 50$

Biology as a predictor. Biology grades were found to be significantly correlated with the catering results. Students with grades 1 and 2 had a strong chance of obtaining a credit, grades 3 and 4 gave no very clear indication either way, and students ungraded or awarded grade 5 had a relatively poor chance of obtaining a credit. If biology grades had been interpreted in this way, the further education results of 27 per cent of these students would have been predicted correctly, with 62 per cent in the 'don't know' category.

52

Table 5.8 Performance of students with CSE biology

Grade	1	2	3	4	5 & U	Total
Credit	5 (17) 12		17	15	3	52
Below credit	0 (8) 8		13	19	11	51
Total	5 (25) 20		30	34	14	103
% in each grade with credit	68		57	44	21	

$C = ·29$ $·05 > P > ·01$

General science as a predictor. General science was found to be one of the best predictors of this course. A threshold was evident below grade 3: students with this grade or above had a strong expectation of reaching the credit level, and those below it a relatively poor chance. If the students with grade 3 and above had been predicted to pass with credit, and the others predicted not to, 75 per cent of the predictions would have been correct. The potential usefulness of general science was somewhat displaced, however, by the fact that fewer students had taken this subject than any other CSE subject investigated in connexion with the general catering course: the predictive information yielded by grades in this subject is unlikely to be available for the majority of the students who take this course.

Table 5.9 Performance of students with CSE general science

Grade	1	2	3	4	5 & U	Total
Credit	1	2	12	4	1	20
		(15)		(5)		
Below credit	0	3	3	14	4	24
		(6)		(18)		
Total		21		23		44
% in each grade with credit		71		22		

$C = ·45$ $·01 > P$

Art as a predictor. There was no evidence that art grades could have given any indication of how students would perform on the catering course.

Table 5.10 Performance of students with CSE art

Grade	1	2	3	4	5 & U		Total
Credit	10	12	9	4	(7)	3	38
Below credit	11	7	14	17	(21)	4	53
Total	21	19	23	28			91
% in each grade with credit	48	63	39	25			

C = ·28   ·10 > P > ·05

Predicting performance on the general catering course from combined pairs of CSE subjects. The sample was divided by random processes into a development group and a trial group, the former comprising two-thirds of the students. Five pairs of CSE subjects were chosen for investigation as multiple predictors. Using the data of the development group, discriminant functions were calculated for the purpose of classifying students into either a 'credit' or a 'below credit' category. It will be seen from Table 5.11 that in three cases the weight assigned in the dis-

Table 5.11 Discriminant functions for predicting performance on the general catering course

Combined subjects	Weights	Mean D-scores		
		Credit or above	Below credit	Cut-off point
English and mathematics	0·636 0·092	*	*	*
Mathematics and history	0·303 0·114	1·474	1·686	1·200
History and geography	0·021 0·355	*	*	*
Geography and domestic science	0·350 0·285	1·690	1·981	1·835
English and history	0·648 0·091	*	*	*

* not calculated

54

criminant function to one of the combined subjects was small. In these cases the discriminant function analysis was taken no further.

In order to test their validity as predictors, the discriminant functions for mathematics and history and for geography and domestic science were applied to students in the trial group. The proportion of correct predictions each discriminant function made was compared with the proportion it would have made had it been predicting merely by a process of random classification. The significance of the improvement on random classification was then found (Table 5.12). Only one of the combinations, geography with domestic science, classified the students into 'credit and above' and 'below credit' categories significantly better than if it had been doing so merely at random.

Table 5.12 Validity of the two discriminant functions for predicting performance on the general catering course

Combined subjects	Number of students in the trial group	Proportion of these students whose results were correctly predicted (%)
Mathematics and history	30	67
Geography and domestic science	24	75*

* an improvement on random classification significant at the 5 per cent level

The one significant discriminant function predicted with a respectable degree of efficiency. The majority of the students whom it classified as likely to obtain a credit did so, and the majority of those whom it classified as unlikely to reach this standard were also classified correctly. These figures are broken down in Table 5.13. However, it must be stressed that this result is based on the performance of only twenty-four students, and ought therefore to be accepted with caution.

Table 5.13 Efficiency of the discriminant function of geography and domestic science for predicting performance on the general catering course

	Credit	Below credit
Predicted to obtain credit	10	2
Predicted to be below credit	4	8

6. Ladies' hairdressing course

Summary of results

Two of the seven CSE subjects investigated were found to predict performance on the hairdressing course (City and Guilds Subject 263) – domestic science and English. The former of these gave the stronger prediction.

Grade	Chances in 100 of a result ←Below credit—————————————Credit or above→	Chances of credit or above
DOMESTIC SCIENCE		
1, 2		96
3		71
4, 5, & *U*		40
ENGLISH		
1		88
2		78
3		64
4, 5, & *U*		56

Fig. 6.1. Chances in 100 of passing with credit on the ladies' hairdressing course associated with each grade in CSE domestic science and English.

Analysis of the data

There were 200 students in the sample, comprising the returns from thirty-four colleges. Ninety per cent of these students were following full-time courses, most of the students studying hairdressing under apprenticeship schemes having apparently left school before taking CSE. Eighty-five per cent of the sample were girls, and most had taken CSE in 1968, immediately before beginning the college course.

56

The examinations in ladies' hairdressing have a very high pass-rate. It was clear that since only 2 per cent of the sample failed, it would have been pointless to evaluate CSE for its capacity to distinguish between the students who would pass and those who would fail. The alternative was to inquire whether CSE grades could have been used to identify the 'high flyers' who would pass with credit, the proportion of the sample who did so being 71 per cent. For the purposes of the analysis, therefore, the students were grouped into 'credit and above' and 'below credit' categories.

Seven CSE subjects were studied as possible predictors: English, mathematics, geography, domestic science, needlework, biology, and art. Numbers were small, and so it was often necessary to combine grades to make a statistical analysis possible. Shortage of data also restricted the analysis to one multiple predictor: English combined with mathematics.

English as a predictor. English grades were significantly correlated with performance in the hairdressing examination – the higher the grade, the greater the probability of gaining a credit. However, there is no evidence in the data given in Table 6.1 to suggest that English grades could have been used to distinguish between the 'high flyers' and the others. Even the students with grade 4 or below, who possessed the poorest chance of reaching the credit level, were more likely to obtain credits than not.

Table 6.1 Performance of students with CSE English

Grade	1	2	3	4		5 & U	Total
Credit or above	15	32	25	21	(27)	6	99
Below credit	2	9	14	18	(21)	3	46
Total	17	41	39		48		145
% in each grade with credit or above	88	78	64		56		

$C = \cdot24$ $\quad \cdot05 > P > \cdot01$

Mathematics as a predictor. There was no evidence of a connexion between performance in C S E mathematics and performance in the hairdressing examination.

Table 6.2 Performance of students with C S E mathematics

Grade	1	2	3	4	5 & U	Total
Credit or above	2 (16)	14	19	33	29	97
Below credit	1 (4)	3	4	7	9	24
Total		20	23	40	38	121
% in each grade with credit or above		80	83	83	76	

$C = \cdot 07$ $\cdot 95 > P > \cdot 80$

Geography as a predictor. There was no evidence that geography grades could have been used to predict performance in the hairdressing examination.

Table 6.3 Performance of students with C S E geography

Grade	1	2	3	4	5 & U	Total
Credit or above	2 (10)	8	9	17	6	42
Below credit	0 (4)	4	7	3	5	19
Total		14	16	20	11	61
% in each grade with credit or above		71	56	85	55	

$C = \cdot 28$ $\cdot 25 > P > \cdot 10$

Domestic science as a predictor. The data collected suggest the presence of a strong correlation between domestic science grades and the hairdressing results. Each increase in a grade was matched by an increase in the probability of passing at the credit standard. Domestic science thus emerged as the best predictor among the seven CSE subjects investigated.

Table 6.4 Performance of students with CSE domestic science

Grade	1	2	3	4	5 & U		Total
Credit or above	6 (25)	19	10	9 (10)	1		45
Below credit	0 (1)	1	4	9 (15)	6		20
Total	26		14	25			65
% in each grade with credit or above	96		71	40			

$C = \cdot54 \qquad \cdot01 > P$

Needlework as a predictor. There was no indication in the data collected that needlework possessed predictive value.

Table 6.5 Performance of students with CSE needlework

Grade	1	2	3	4	5 & U		Total
Credit or above	5 (18)	13	9	6	(6) 0		33
Below credit	2 (6)	4	2	4	(7) 3		15
Total	24		11	13			48
% in each grade with credit or above	75		82	46			

$C = \cdot31 \qquad \cdot25 > P > \cdot10$

59

Biology as a predictor. Biology showed no evidence of possessing predictive value.

Table 6.6 Performance of students with CSE biology

Grade	1	2	3	4	5 & U	Total
Credit or above	4 (15)	11	11	14	7	47
Below credit	2 (4)	2	5	7	6	22
Total		19	16	21	13	69
% in each grade with credit or above		79	68	67	54	

C = ·19   ·50 > P > ·25

Art as a predictor. There was no evidence in the data collected to suggest that grades in art could have been used to predict performance in the hairdressing examination.

Table 6.7 Performance of students with CSE art

Grade	1	2	3	4	5 & U	Total
Credit or above	13	10	12	(10) 11	(1)	46
Below credit	3	5	8	(3) 4	(1)	20
Total	16	15	20	15		66
% in each grade with credit or above	81	67	60	73		

C = ·18   ·75 > P > ·50

Predicting performance on the hairdressing course from combined grades in English and mathematics. Eighty-four students had taken both English and mathematics. They were divided by random processes into a development group of fifty-nine and a trial group of twenty-five. A discriminant function was calculated from the data in the development group, giving weights of 0·666 for English and 0·275 for mathematics. The mean weighted score for the students obtaining a credit or higher was 2·980 and for those who did not attain this standard 3·779. The cut-off point was located at 3·580.

The discriminant function was then applied to the 25 students in the trial group in order to estimate its efficiency of prediction. It correctly predicted the results of seventeen (68 per cent) of these. On the hypothesis that the discriminant function was selecting the 'credit and above' and the 'below credit' groups merely at random, however, we should expect 73 per cent of them to have been correctly predicted. The efficiency trial therefore gave no evidence that the discriminant function was making genuine predictions at all.

Conclusions

The best predictor of performance on the hairdressing course was domestic science. English also gave an indication of students' chances of attaining the credit level, but the correlation was much lower. The practical utility of these results is somewhat reduced, however, because it is the custom for hairdressing apprentices to commence their training at the age of 15. Only those who choose to take the City and Guilds course full-time customarily stay on at school for CSE.

7. Shorthand-typists' certificate, stage II

Summary of results

Eight CSE subjects were investigated for their predictive validity. There was no clear indication that any of them could have been used to predict performance on this RSA course.

Analysis of the data

The sample comprised 227 girls in twenty-eight colleges of further education. Most were studying full-time, and most had begun the college course immediately after leaving school. Forty-nine per cent passed shorthand-typing, stage II. The aim of the investigation was to discover whether, by referring to their CSE grades, these students could be distinguished from those who failed. Eight CSE subjects were investigated as possible predictors: English, mathematics, history, geography, biology, a modern foreign language, typewriting, and domestic science. The predictive value of combinations of these subjects was not studied, because too few students had taken even the most popular combinations to make such an investigation worth while.

English as a predictor. No evidence was found of a connexion between grades in English and the RSA results.

Table 7.1 Performance of students with CSE English

Grade	1	2	3	4	5 & U		Total
Passed	19	20	5	4	(4)	0	48
Failed	29	16	13	5	(7)	2	65
Total	48	36	18		11		113
% in each grade who passed	40	56	28		36		

$C = \cdot 22$ $\cdot 20 > P > \cdot 10$

Mathematics as a predictor. There was a significant correlation between mathematics grades and performance in the RSA examinations, but the relationship was irregular among the lower grades. Students with grades 1 and 2 had a good chance of passing, and those with grade 3 or below a relatively poor chance. If students with grade 2 and above had been predicted to pass, and those with grade 3 and below predicted to fail, the results of 65 per cent of the sample would have been predicted correctly.

Table 7.2 Performance of students with CSE mathematics

Grade	1	2	3	4	5 & U	Total
Passed	16	16	12	20	5	69
Failed	4	11	23	30	10	78
Total	20	27	35	50	15	147
% in each grade who passed	80	59	34	40	33	

$C = \cdot 32$ $\cdot 01 > P$

It is difficult to explain why mathematics grades should have predicted the performance of shorthand-typing students, as the RSA syllabus does not include mathematics. Possibly, the CSE results reflected the presence of aptitudes important for success in shorthand-typing, such as the ability to manipulate an artificial language of symbols. But without research in greater depth this must remain conjectural, and so the apparent predictive validity of mathematics should be regarded with caution.

History as a predictor. There were no indications that history grades could have been used to predict performance in the shorthand-typing examinations.

Table 7.3 Performance of students with CSE history

Grade	1	2	3	4	5 & U		Total
Passed	8	11	7	3	(5)	2	31
Failed	7	8	8	7	(11)	4	34
Total	15	19	15		16		65
% in each grade who passed	53	58	47		31		

$C = \cdot20$ $\cdot50 > P > \cdot25$

Geography as a predictor. No evidence was found of a connexion between geography grades and the RSA results.

Table 7.4 Performance of students with CSE geography

Grade	1	2	3	4	5 & U	Total
Passed	7	9	6	7	5	34
Failed	7	9	13	9	6	44
Total	14	18	19	16	11	78
% in each grade who passed	50	50	32	44	46	

$C = \cdot15$ $\cdot80 > P > \cdot70$

Biology as a predictor. There was no apparent connexion between grades in biology and the shorthand-typing results.

Table 7.5 Performance of students with CSE biology

Grade	1	2	3	4	5 & U	Total
Passed	3 (8)	5	5	6 (8)	2	21
Failed	6 (12)	6	10	7 (8)	1	30
Total	20		15	16		51
% in each grade who passed	40		33	50		

$C = \cdot13$ $\quad\quad \cdot75 > P > \cdot50$

A modern foreign language as a predictor. Grades in French, German, and Spanish were included under this heading. They gave the second largest correlation with the shorthand-typing results, but it was nevertheless too small to be significant.

Table 7.6 Performance of students with CSE in a modern foreign language

Grade	1	2	3	4	5 & U	Total
Passed	17	9	8	6 (6)	0	40
Failed	8	9	11	7 (12)	5	40
Total	25	18	19	18		80
% in each grade who passed	68	50	42	33		

$C = \cdot27$ $\quad\quad \cdot25 > P > \cdot10$

Typewriting as a predictor. No evidence was found to suggest that typewriting grades could have been used to predict the RSA results.

Table 7.7 Performance of students with CSE typewriting

Grade	1	2	3	4	5 & U			Total
Passed	7	3	6	4	(7)	3		23
Failed	8	8	7	3	(5)	2		28
Total	15	11	13	12				51
% in each grade who passed	47	27	46	58				

$C = \cdot21$ $\cdot75 > P > \cdot50$

Domestic science as a predictor. There was no evidence of a correlation between domestic science grades and the shorthand-typing results.

Table 7.8 Performance of students with CSE domestic science

Grade	1	2	3	4	5 & U			Total
Passed	8	5	6	3	(6)	3		25
Failed	9	13	8	4	(4)	0		34
Total	17	18	14	10				59
% in each grade who passed	47	28	43	60				

$C = \cdot23$ $\cdot50 > P > \cdot25$

Conclusions

Little evidence emerged during the course of the investigation to suggest that CSE results could have yielded information concerning students' chances of success on the shorthand-typing course. A possible explanation is that their school attainment was unrelated to their performance on this particular course, and that the best way of detecting ability for shorthand-typing would have been to use special diagnostic tests. The only explanation for the apparent predictive value of mathematics is that it served in this guise as an indirect measure of an aptitude for learning an artificial language of symbols. It was unfortunately not possible to collect sufficient data to allow a study of CSE shorthand-typing, which had the strongest face validity as a predictor for this further education course.

8. Secretarial duties, stage II

Summary of results

Seven of the nine CSE subjects investigated could have been used to predict the examination performance of the students in the sample. They were: business studies, biology, history, domestic science, geography, mathematics, and English. The best predictions were given by the first three of these. A combination of mathematics and geography also gave good predictions, but its usefulness should be accepted with caution as it was tested on a relatively small sample.

Analysis of the data

The 251 secretarial students in the sample were all female, all full-time, and the majority had taken CSE immediately before beginning their college course. Fifty-one per cent passed the RSA examination. The purpose of the statistical analysis was to test whether, by referring to their CSE grades, these students could have been distinguished from those who failed. Nine individual CSE subjects were investigated for their predictive value: English, mathematics, history, geography, biology, modern foreign languages, business studies, type-writing, and domestic science. Two pairs of these were investigated as possible multiple predictors: English combined with mathematics, and mathematics combined with geography. Numbers were too small to allow other combinations to be studied.

English as a predictor. English grades were significantly correlated with the results of the RSA examination. Each increase of a grade was associated with an increase in the probability of passing.

Table 8.1 Performance of students with CSE English

Grade	1	2	3	4	5 & U	Total
Passed	30	17	6	3 (3)	0	56
Failed	25	26	18	9 (11)	2	80
Total	55	43	24	14		136
% in each grade who passed	55	40	25	21		

$C = \cdot 26$ $\cdot 05 > P > \cdot 025$

There was no evidence, however, that grades in English could have been used with much efficiency to distinguish those who would pass from those who would fail. The higher grades were not associated very strongly with success, the

66

Chances in 100 of

Grade	←—Failing————————————————————Passing—→	Chances of passing

BUSINESS STUDIES

Grade		Chances of passing
1 & 2		86
3, 4, 5, & U		17

BIOLOGY

Grade		Chances of passing
1		89
2		80
3		57
4, 5, & U		14

HISTORY

Grade		Chances of passing
1		88
2		59
3		33
4, 5, & U		28

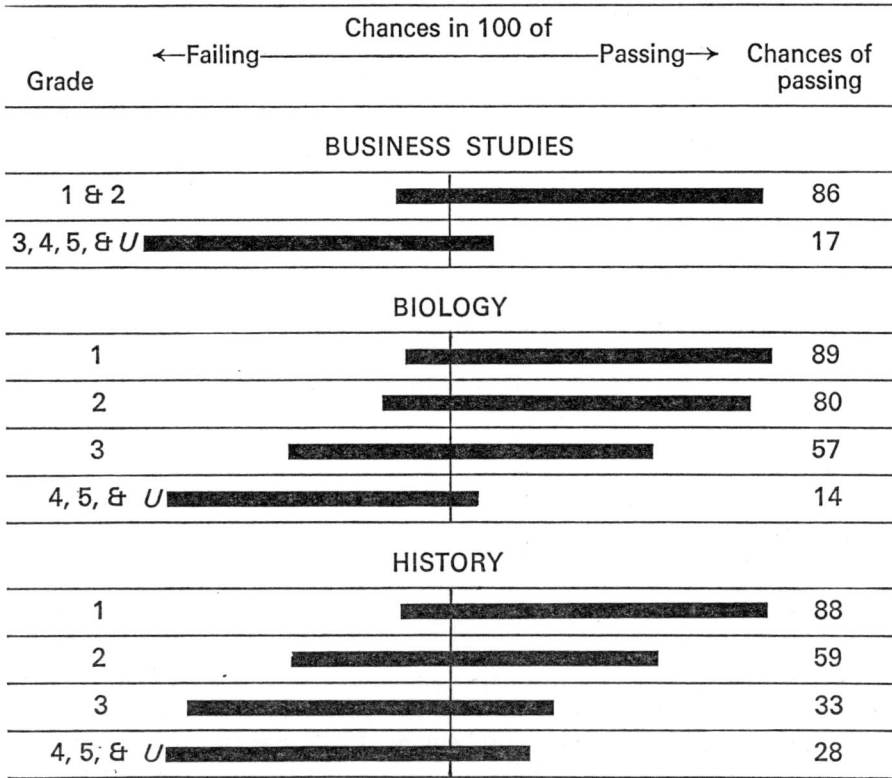

Fig. 8.1. Chances in 100 of passing the secretrial duties course associated with each grade in business studies, biology, and history.

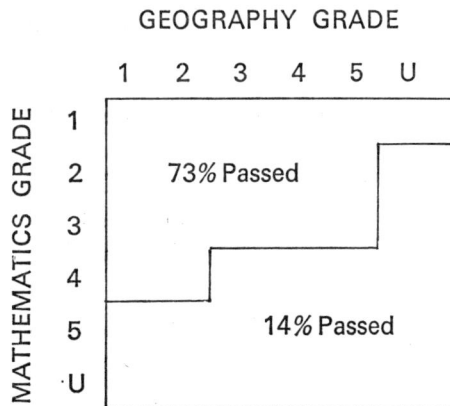

GEOGRAPHY GRADE

1 2 3 4 5 U

MATHEMATICS GRADE

1 2 3 4 5 U

73% Passed

14% Passed

Fig. 8.2. Proportions passing the secretarial duties course with various combinations of CSE grades in mathematics and geography.

students with grade 1 having had only 55 chances in 100 of passing and there were few low grades in the sample, obscuring their predictive implications. There are signs that the probability of success decreased among students with grade 4 and below, but numbers were too small to allow much to be inferred with confidence. The relative absence of students with the lower grades was perhaps because the selection process was partly based on students' English attainment.

Mathematics as a predictor. Mathematics grades were significantly correlated with the further education results.

Table 8.2 Performance of students with CSE mathematics

Grade	1	2	3	4	5 & U	Total
Passed	22	22	23	21	9	97
Failed	6	12	18	25	14	75
Total	28	34	41	46	23	172
% in each grade who passed	79	65	56	46	39	

$C = \cdot 26$ $\qquad \cdot 05 > P > \cdot 02$

Students with grade 3 or above were more likely to pass than to fail, and those with grade 4 or below were more likely to fail than to pass. However, the lower grades did not indicate as strong a probability of failure as the upper grades did of success. If students with grade 3 or above had been predicted to pass, and the others to fail, the results of 62 per cent of these students would have been predicted correctly.

History as a predictor. There was a highly significant correlation between history grades and the RSA results.

Table 8.3 Performance of students with CSE history

Grade	1	2	3	4	5 & U		Total
Passed	15	13	5	5	(5)	0	38
Failed	2	9	10	9	(13)	4	34
Total	17	22	15		18		72
% in each grade who passed	88	59	33		28		

$C = \cdot 47$ $\qquad \cdot 01 > P$

Students with grade 2 or above were more likely to pass than to fail, and those with grade 3 and below were more likely to fail than to pass. If the former group had been predicted to pass and the latter to fail, the results of 70 per cent of the students would have been predicted correctly.

Geography as a predictor. Geography proved to be a valid predictor.

Table 8.4 Performance of students with CSE geography

Grade	1	2	3	4	5 & U	Total
Passed	9	8	10	7	3	37
Failed	2	8	13	17	8	48
Total	11	16	23	24	11	85
% in each grade who passed	82	50	44	29	27	

$C = \cdot34$ $\quad \cdot05 > P > \cdot02$

Students with grade 1 had a high expectation of success; there was no clear indication either way for those with grades 2 and 3, and those with grade 4 and below were likely to fail. If those with grade 1 had been predicted to pass and those with grade 4 and below to fail, 40 per cent of the predictions would have been correct, with 46 per cent in the 'don't know' category.

Biology as a predictor. A highly significant correlation was evident between biology grades and the further education results.

Table 8.5 Performance of students with CSE biology

Grade	1	2	3	4	5 & U		Total
Passed	8	12	13	3	(3)	0	36
Failed	1	3	10	12	(18)	6	32
Total	9	15	23		21		68
% in each grade who passed	89	80	57		14		

$C = \cdot57$ $\quad \cdot01 > P$

Grades 1 and 2 were associated with a strong probability of success. Students with grade 3 had more chance of passing than of failing, but the difference was only marginal. Students with grade 4 and below were likely to fail. If grades 1 and 2 had been taken to predict success and grade 4 and below to predict failure, the results of 56 per cent of these students would have been predicted correctly, and 34 per cent would have been placed in the 'don't know' category.

A modern foreign language as a predictor. French, German, and Spanish were grouped together under this heading. There was no evidence of a correlation between grades in these subjects and performance in the secretarial duties examination.

Table 8.6 Performance of students with CSE in a modern foreign language

Grade	1	2	3	4	5 & U		Total
Passed	18	12	16	9	(10)	1	56
Failed	7	9	11	7	(9)	2	36
Total	25	21	27	19			92
% in each grade who passed	72	57	59	53			

C = ·15   ·75 > P > ·50

Business studies as a predictor. A number of subjects which could be described as 'business studies' were grouped together: commerce, accounts, and book-keeping. The sub-sample was small, making it necessary to group the grades into two categories: grade 2 and above, and grade 3 and below. Treated in this way, business studies grades proved to have high predictive validity.

Table 8.7 Performance of students with CSE business studies

Grade	1	2	3	4	5 & U	Total
Passed	7 (12)	5	2	3	0	17
				(5)		
Failed	1 (2)	1	9	10	5	26
				(24)		
Total	14			29		43
% in each grade who passed	86			17		

C = ·61   ·01 > P

The upper grades implied a high expectation of passing, the lower grades a poor one. If the performance of the students in the sample had been predicted on this basis, the results of 84 per cent would have been predicted correctly. Business studies subjects thus emerged as the best predictors of performance on the secretarial duties course, but because few students had taken one of these subjects, this predictive information is unlikely to be available for the majority of the students.

Typewriting as a predictor. There was no evidence that typewriting grades had predictive validity.

Table 8.8 Performance of students with CSE typewriting

Grade	1	2	3	4	5 & U		Total
Passed	6	7	6	3	(4)	1	23
Failed	5	6	8	9	(13)	4	32
Total	11	13	14		17		55
% in each grade who passed	55	54	43		24		

$C = \cdot 27 \qquad \cdot 50 > P > \cdot 25$

Domestic science as a predictor. Grades in domestic science were significantly correlated with the results of the secretarial duties examination.

Table 8.9 Performance of students with CSE domestic science

Grade	1	2	3	4	5 & U		Total
Passed	10	11	8	3	(3)	0	32
Failed	2	10	11	7	(8)	1	31
Total	12	21	19		11		63
% in each grade who passed	83	52	42		27		

$C = \cdot 36 \qquad \cdot 05 > P > \cdot 025$

Grade 1 implied a good chance of passing, grades 2 and 3 gave no clear indication either way, and grades 4 and below implied a likelihood of failing. If the performance of these students had been predicted on the above interpretations, the results of 29 per cent would have been predicted correctly, with 63 per cent in the 'don't know' category.

Predicting performance on the secretarial duties course from combined pairs of CSE subjects. The sample was divided by random processes into a development group and a trial group, comprising two-thirds and one-third of the sample respectively. Discriminant functions were calculated for the two pairs of subjects to be investigated as possible multiple predictors, using the data of the development group (Table 8.10).

Table 8.10 Discriminant functions for predicting performance on the secretarial duties course

| Combined subjects | Weights | Mean D-scores | | Cut-off point |
		Passed	Failed	
English and mathematics	0·316 0·493	2·092	2·689	2·390
Mathematics and geography	0·652 0·241	2·744	3·634	3·189

The predictive validity of the two discriminant functions was tested by applying them to the students in the trial group. The proportion of correct predictions made by each was compared with the proportion it would have made had it been predicting merely by a process of random classification. The significance of the improvement on random classification was then found (Table 8.11).

Table 8.11 Validity of the discriminant functions for predicting performance on the secretarial duties course

Combined subjects	Number of students in the trial group	Proportion of these whose results were correctly predicted (%)
English and mathematics	31	65
Mathematics and geography	18	78*

* an improvement on random classification significant at the 5 per cent level

Using the proportion of correct predictions as a criterion of efficiency, the better multiple predictor appears to have been the combination of mathematics and geography. This combination was also as successful in identifying those students who would pass the secretarial duties examination as it was in identifying those who would fail – the combination of English and mathematics successfully performed only the latter of these two functions (Table 8.12). However, it must be emphasized that these results are based on a small quantity of data, and so the predictive value of mathematics combined with geography should be accepted cautiously.

Table 8.12 Efficiency of the discriminant functions for predicting performance on the secretarial duties course

| | English and mathematics | | Mathematics and geography | |
	Passed	*Failed*	*Passed*	*Failed*
Predicted to pass	9	8	8	3
Predicted to fail	3	11	1	6

Conclusions

Most of the CSE subjects investigated could have been used to predict performance in the secretarial duties examination. The reason why so many subjects proved to possess predictive value is probably that the secretarial duties syllabus includes a wide range of skills, such as writing letters and reports, preparing charts and graphs, calculating wages, and other activities, for which an all-round rather than a specialized education would appear to be the best preparation.

IV. General conclusions

The findings of this research can be summarized as follows.

Could anything have been inferred from students' CSE grades about their chances of success in further education? We found that students' college performance could have been predicted in all but one of the eight further education courses investigated. How much reliance could have been placed on this predictive information? It is notoriously difficult to decide how large a correlation must be in order to possess practical utility, and in this case the best criterion – comparison with alternative predictive measures – is unavailable. The final judgement on the usefulness of CSE must therefore wait until more is known of the predictive validity of such measures as interviews and headteachers' reports. However, the correlations obtained were in general too low to justify prediction on the basis of CSE alone. Where CSE results possess predictive value, they must be used as supplementary information.

Which CSE subjects were the best predictors? It was usually possible to identify one or two subjects as the best predictors of each course. The procedure of comparing the correlations for different subjects was not infallible, for it was evident that the students on certain courses had been selected by their grades in some but not all of the CSE subjects they had taken. The resulting differential restriction of range would have distorted the relative strength of the correlations. However, instances of severe restriction of range were few, and it is unlikely that much information has been lost due to the operation of this factor.

What probability of success was associated with each grade in the subjects with predictive value? Two general points arise from the evaluation of individual grades in terms of implied chances of success in further education. First, in many cases the increase in the probability of success associated with each increase of a grade was gradual: in these cases it would have been arbitrary to select one grade as a minimum entry requirement. Second, the strength with which high grades were associated with success and the strength with which low grades were associated with failure were not always commensurate with one another. On the engineering craft studies course, for instance, high grades indicated a high expectation of passing with credit, but low grades indicated no worse than an even chance of attaining this standard.

In drawing these conclusions, the results of Chapter III have been interpreted as a general and tentative indication of the extent to which CSE possesses predictive value – a basis for further research and development. An alternative way of interpreting them would be to accept them as a detailed account of how CSE results are to be used in the everyday problems of vocational guidance and selection. It must be emphasized that the direct use of the results of Chapter III for these purposes would involve generalizing them from the students on whom the research was conducted to others, and that any systematic differences between the two groups would give rise to error. It is recognized, however, that the exigencies of allocating students to further education courses have created a demand for detailed information which can be used immediately. We therefore suggest that if colleges and employers utilize the detailed information of Chapter III, they should perform validation studies to keep a constant check on the procedures adopted.

The Crowther Report criticized the 'lack of integration between the education that students receive in the technical colleges and the education they have received at school . . . we believe that the boy coming from a school into a technical college is entitled to have his transition from the one institution to the other as carefully thought out and watched over as the transition of the sixth former to the university should be .'* The Newsom Report stressed the 'double need for information, both in the selection of a boy or girl for a job which may be associated, we hope increasingly, with a course of training or part-time education; and in direct selection for courses by technical institutions. Here personal links between the college principals and the schools are essential.'† This project, of itself an exercise in co-operation between the secondary and further education sectors, has underlined the advantages of such co-operation in the important matter of implementing the conviction expressed in the 1944 Education Act that education should be a continuing process. It has sought to fill in some of the gaps in the mutual understanding between secondary and further education, without which a smooth transition between the two cannot be effected.

While showing that CSE can provide additional information for allocating students to further education courses, the findings of this project confirm the prescience of the Beloe Report in thinking it important that 'ways should be left open for those who are not able to show their quality in terms of school examination results.'‡ Students with low CSE grades possessed a high chance of success on a number of the further education courses investigated. Sixty-five per cent of the students ungraded or awarded grade 5 in mathematics, for instance, subsequently passed the craft studies course with credit. It cannot be said that the opportunities of further education are closed to those who perform badly in CSE.

* *15 to 18:* a report of the Central Advisory Council for Education (England) (HMSO, 1959), para. 526.

† *Half Our Future:* a report of the Central Advisory Council for Education (England) (HMSO, 1963), para. 257.

‡ *Secondary School Examinations other than the GCE* (HMSO, 1960), para. 133.

Appendices

Appendix A Supplementary tables*

Table A.1.1 CSE subjects investigated as possible predictors for the mechanical technicians course

Subject	N	Mean	Standard deviation	% passing mechanical technicians examination
English	735	3·19	1·13	72
Mathematics	810	2·88	1·26	73
Technical drawing	640	2·56	1·24	73
Physics	406	3·14	1·18	77
Metalwork	405	2·43	1·24	75
Geography	414	2·93	1·21	74
History	256	3·22	1·27	75
General science	195	2·93	1·20	70

Table A.1.2 CSE subjects investigated as possible predictors of the mechanical technicians course: heterogeneity of the sub-samples

Subject	Mode of further education study		Year of taking CSE				
	Part-time	Block release	65	66	67	68	69
English	663	72	18	66	195	437	19
Mathematics	727	83	19	70	219	481	21
Technical drawing	574	66	14	67	176	369	14
Physics	367	39	5	27	104	259	11
Metalwork	364	41	12	35	100	250	8
Geography	369	45	9	36	112	247	10
History	227	29	8	22	61	157	8
General science	166	29	12	24	49	108	2

* In calculating means and standard deviations, the ungraded result has been scored as 6.

Table A.2.1 CSE subjects investigated as possible predictors of the electrical technicians course

Subject	N	Mean	Standard deviation	% passing electrical technicians course
English	301	3·24	1·03	62
Mathematics	309	2·87	1·22	61
Technical drawing	225	2·67	1·30	60
Physics	220	2·99	1·13	63
Metalwork	129	2·76	1·26	55
Woodwork	88	2·92	1·25	67
Geography	184	2·91	1·24	63
History	105	3·32	1·39	60
General science	61	2·67	1·56	54

Table A.2.2 CSE subjects investigated as possible predictors of the electrical technicians course: heterogeneity of the sub-samples

Subject	Mode of further education study			Year of taking CSE				
	Full-time	Part-time	Block release	65	66	67	68	69
English	16	272	13	9	55	98	122	17
Mathematics	14	281	14	8	53	101	132	15
Technical drawing	10	203	12	5	37	76	96	11
Physics	11	197	12	4	28	77	98	13
Metalwork	5	122	2	5	23	36	60	5
Woodwork	4	79	5	2	16	40	26	4
Geography	8	168	8	4	31	65	75	9
History	2	98	5	5	17	30	50	3
General science	2	57	2	5	14	15	26	1

Table A.3.1 CSE subjects investigated as possible predictors of the general course in engineering

Subject	N	Mean	Standard deviation	% qualified for entry to ONC	Full-time	Part-time	Block release
					Mode of further education study		
English	356	2·96	1·09	31	64	242	50
Mathematics	368	2·47	1·26	30	64	255	49
Technical drawing	276	2·39	1·28	31	53	185	38
Physics	253	2·74	1·10	32	40	168	45
Metalwork	154	2·28	1·25	32	28	104	22
Woodwork	115	2·20	1·15	24	24	71	20
Geography	217	2·63	1·22	33	44	144	29
History	138	2·95	1·32	35	25	88	25
General science	67	2·24	1·05	33	20	42	5

Table A.4.1 CSE subjects investigated as possible predictors of the basic craft studies course

Subject	N	Mean	Standard deviation	% passing craft studies examination with credit or distinction
Metalwork	498	2·59	1·26	82
Woodwork	277	2·70	1·14	80
Mathematics	880	3·70	1·37	82
Geography	523	3·43	1·25	79
History	356	3·73	1·31	75
General science	199	3·38	1·33	83
English	894	3·59	1·11	81
Technical drawing	701	3·19	1·44	85
Physics	522	3·68	1·17	87

Table A.4.2 CSE subjects investigated as possible predictors of the basic craft studies course: heterogeneity of the sub-samples

Subject	Mode of further education study			Year of taking CSE		
	Full-time	Part-time	Block release	67	68	69
Metalwork	144	327	28	5	26	467
Woodwork	82	178	18	2	18	257
Mathematics	265	559	59	6	46	828
Geography	150	340	36	4	24	495
History	107	228	25	3	15	338
General science	67	114	18	—	10	189
English	272	568	57	7	46	841
Technical drawing	227	434	41	4	41	656
Physics	166	324	32	5	19	498

Table A.5.1 CSE subjects investigated as possible predictors of the general catering course

Subject	N	Mean	Standard deviation	% passing with credit	Year of taking CSE 67	68	69	Sex F	M
English	309	3·17	1·14	42	4	18	287	166	143
Mathematics	255	3·89	1·23	42	3	14	238	131	124
History	151	3·48	1·28	39	5	9	137	71	80
Geography	170	3·22	1·24	42	3	10	157	90	80
Domestic science	150	2·45	1·12	51	2	4	144	129	21
Foreign language	63	3·49	1·33	51	1	4	58	34	29
Needlework	62	2·85	1·22	56	1	3	58	61	1
Biology	103	3·34	1·14	50	—	6	97	73	30
General science	44	3·50	0·97	45	2	1	41	15	29
Art	91	2·74	1·31	42	2	4	85	43	48

Table A.6.1 CSE subjects investigated as possible predictors of the ladies' hairdressing course

Subject	N	Mean	Standard deviation	% passing with credit
English	145	2·88	1·13	68
Mathematics	121	3·89	1·28	80
Geography	61	3·49	1·21	69
Domestic science	65	3·02	1·21	69
Needlework	48	2·71	1·19	69
Biology	69	3·36	1·30	68
Art	66	2·55	1·14	70

Table A.6.2 CSE subjects investigated as possible predictors of the ladies' hairdressing course: heterogeneity of the sub-samples

Subject	Mode of further education study		Year of taking CSE				Sex	
	Full-time	Part-time	65	66	67	68	F	M
English	134	11	1	4	16	124	132	13
Mathematics	107	14	2	2	21	96	110	11
Geography	54	7	—	2	12	47	54	7
Domestic science	60	5	1	1	6	57	65	—
Needlework	42	6	—	3	7	38	47	1
Biology	63	6	1	1	7	60	66	3
Art	65	1	—	—	5	61	60	6

Table A.7.1 CSE subjects investigated as possible predictors of the shorthand-typists' course

Subject	N	Mean	Standard deviation	Pass-rate in further education	Year of taking CSE				
					65	66	67	68	69
English	113	1·94	1·02	42	—	1	4	39	69
Mathematics	147	3·12	1·26	47	1	1	11	54	80
History	65	2·60	1·29	48	—	1	3	25	36
Geography	78	2·93	1·32	44	—	1	3	28	46
Biology	51	2·82	1·22	41	—	1	3	22	25
Foreign language	80	2·45	1·27	50	1	—	5	24	50
Typewriting	51	2·55	1·35	45	—	—	1	10	40
Domestic science	59	2·36	1·20	42	—	—	1	21	37

Table A.8.1 CSE subjects investigated as possible predictors of the secretarial duties course

Subject	N	Mean	Standard deviation	% passing secretarial duties examination	Year of taking CSE 67	Year of taking CSE 68	Year of taking CSE 69
English	136	1·99	1·03	41	1	35	100
Mathematics	172	3·05	1·36	53	7	50	115
History	72	2·54	1·24	53	—	23	49
Geography	85	3·13	1·29	44	1	23	61
Biology	68	2·96	1·24	47	1	16	51
Foreign language	92	2·47	1·16	61	4	26	62
Business studies	43	2·67	1·20	54	1	10	32
Typewriting	55	2·78	1·29	42	1	7	47
Domestic science	63	2·48	1·02	51	1	20	42

Appendix B Explanation of some of the statistical terms

Correlation: the rationale of the research methods used was that CSE grades can be used to predict the students' further education performance if in general there exists a correlation between CSE grades and the results of the further education examinations. For example, if those who do well in CSE subsequently do well in further education, and those who do badly in CSE do badly in further education, we can gain some advance indication of a student's chances of success in further education by looking at his CSE grades. So the primary task was to look for signs of correlation between CSE subjects and performance in the various further education courses. The strength of an apparent correlation was measured by a coefficient, symbolized by the letter C. This coefficient can take values between 1 and 0, the former representing the complete dependence of further education results upon CSE grades, the latter representing complete independence. Thus $C = \cdot35$ indicates a stronger dependence than $C = \cdot20$.

Significance: even where school and further education performance are independent, a correlation between CSE grades and college results might appear merely by chance. It is possible to determine the probability that a given correlation is merely the result of chance, and if this probability is less than 5 per cent ($\cdot 05 >$ P) the correlation is usually regarded as significant, and as highly significant if the probability of chance occurrence is less than 1 per cent ($\cdot 01 > P$).

Discriminant function: a better prediction is to be expected from combined grades in several CSE subjects than from one CSE subject alone. One way of combining grades is to average them. A more efficient method, however, is to calculate a discriminant function – which is simply a rule for combining several grades into a single score for the purposes of classifying students into two groups. To combine grades in English and mathematics, for example, a weight is determined for each subject, the relative size of the weights reflecting the relative predictive power of the two subjects. Suppose the weight for English is 0·813 and for mathematics 0·412. The method of combining a student's grades in these subjects would be to multiply his grade in each by the respective weight (representing the ungraded result as 6) and then total the results. Thus a student with grade 2 in English and grade 3 in mathematics would score as follows: $(2 \times 0\cdot813) + (3 \times 0\cdot412) = 2\cdot862$. This figure can conveniently be described as his D-score. The weights are determined in such a way that, by reference to their D-scores, the maximum number of students can be correctly classified either as 'will be successful in further education' or as 'will not be successful in further education'. The method by which the students included in the research were so classified was by calculating the average D-score of those who passed, the average D-score of those who failed, and then deciding on a cut-off point somewhere between these two scores. If a student's D-score was between the cut-off point and the average score of those who passed, he was predicted to pass, and if it was on the other side of the cut-off point (that is, nearer the typical score of those who failed), he was predicted to fail.

Appendix C CSE subjects included in the research

In order to obtain sufficiently large samples CSE subjects with slightly different titles had to be grouped together. These groupings are given below. The title used in this report to denote any member of the group is given on the left.

English	English, English language and literature, general English, English language (excluding English literature).
Mathematics	mathematics (excluding modern mathematics, arithmetic, geometry, commercial calculations).
Technical drawing	technical drawing, engineering drawing, geometrical and engineering drawing.
Physics	physics (excluding physics with chemistry, general science).
Metalwork	metalwork, engineering workshop.
Geography	geography (excluding geology, environmental studies).
History	history, economic history.
General science	general science (excluding physics with chemistry).
Biology	biology, human biology, physiology and hygiene.
Chemistry	chemistry (excluding physics with chemistry, general science).
A modern foreign language	French, German, Spanish.
Needlework	needlework, dress.
Business studies	commerce, accounts, book-keeping.
Typewriting	typewriting (excluding shorthand-typing). Only the results from boards issuing them in the form of grades rather than speeds could be used in the research.
Domestic science	domestic science, cookery, homecraft, housecraft, home economics.
Art	art, art and craft.

Members of the consultative committee[*]

D. T. Meyrick (Chairman)	Headmaster, Hassenbrook County Secondary School, Stanford-le-Hope
R. Arnold	HM Inspectorate
D. A. Caruth	Inspector, Essex County Council, Education Office
G. S. Crawshaw	Training Officer, Thames Board Mills Ltd
J. Doughty	District Careers Officer, Grays, Thurrock
J. Evans	Brentwood College of Education
D. J. Gillam	Headmaster, Grays Park County Secondary School, Grays (Chairman, Thurrock CSE Advisory Group)
A. Johnson	Secretary, East Anglian Examinations Board
O. Glyn Jones	Lennard County Secondary School, Ockendon (Secretary, Thurrock CSE Advisory Group)
A. E. Lewis	County Careers Officer, Essex County Council
W. J. W. Preece, MBE	Headmaster, St Chad's County Secondary School, Tilbury
K. J. Razey	District Careers Officer, Grays, Thurrock
F. H. Sparrow	Schools Council

Members of project team

I. C. Williams (project director)	Responsible for Chapters I and IV
N. C. Boreham (project organizer)	Responsible for Chapters II, III and IV

Acknowledgements

The authors are grateful to the following:

Mr F. H. Sparrow, Senior Research Officer, Schools Council, whose advice and encouragment proved invaluable.

The members of the computing division at Thurrock Technical College, for help in data processing.

Mr A. Shaikh, Thurrock Technical College, for advice on statistical matters.

The Director-General of the City and Guilds of London Institute, the Principal of the Examinations Department of the Royal Society of Arts, and their staff for their friendly co-operation in making their examination results available.

[*] The post given is that occupied by the member when the main work was undertaken.

The principals and staff of the hundreds of colleges who helped in the collection of the data.

The members of the consultative committee listed above.

Mrs Delia Pipe, Secretary to the Principal, Thurrock Technical College, who was responsible for all typing connected with the work of the consultative committee, and for the typing of the report.